A NEW ZEALAND CHRISTMAS

A GODWIT BOOK published by
Random House New Zealand
18 Poland Road, Glenfield, Auckland, New Zealand

For more information about our titles go to
www.randomhouse.co.nz

A catalogue record for this book is available from the
National Library of New Zealand

Random House International, Random House, 20 Vauxhall Bridge Road, London, SW1V 2SA, United Kingdom; **Random House Australia Pty Ltd**, Level 3, 100 Pacific Highway, North Sydney 2060, Australia; **Random House South Africa Pty Ltd**, Isle of Houghton, Corner Boundary Road and Carse O'Gowrie, Houghton 2198, South Africa; **Random House Publishers India Private Ltd**, 301 World Trade Tower, Hotel Intercontinental Grand Complex, Barakhamba Lane, New Delhi 110 001, India

First published 2008

© 2008 text, Sarah Ell.
© 2008 images, Alexander Turnbull Library unless otherwise specified.

The moral rights of the author have been asserted

ISBN 978 1 86962 159 9

This book is copyright. Except for the purposes of fair reviewing no part of this publication may be reproduced or transmitted in any form or by any means, electronic or mechanical, including photocopying, recording or any information storage and retrieval system, without permission in writing from the publisher. Every reasonable effort has been undertaken to contact the copyright holders to images contained in this book, and the publishers welcome communication from those who could not be contacted.

Design: Trevor Newman
Printed by South China Printing Co Ltd

Acknowledgements

A big thanks first of all to the wonderful staff at the Alexander Turnbull Library, Wellington, including Barbara Brownlie (Ephemera), Marian Minson (Drawings, Paintings and Prints), Peter Attwell (Research Centre), John Sullivan (Photographic Archive), Amy Watling (Manuscripts and Archives) and Joan McCracken and Chris Szekely.

The second resource I could not have done without is the amazing collections of North Shore Libraries, especially the Takapuna Library and its New Zealand Collection. For every topic I needed to find a book on — and some were pretty obscure — the Takapuna Library seemed to have something that would help. Another fantastic resource I discovered while working on this project is the New Zealand Electronic Text Centre, a free online archive of New Zealand and Pacific Islands texts set up by the Victoria University of Wellington Library, which offers fully searchable versions of hard-to-find and highly useful books, manuscripts and journals. I would never have had the time to find the little details of Christmases experienced by New Zealand soldiers overseas during the Second World War if not for the easy searchability of the NZETC's digital versions of the various volumes of *The Official History of New Zealand in the Second World War 1939–1945*.

Thanks also to Maurice Norton (Takapuna), who sent me his pamphlet on John Philemon Backhouse; Lizzie Catherall (Greytown), for the information on her father, Lieutenant Peter Hamilton; and John Lowry of Ontario, Canada, great-grandson of Benoni Lytton-White, for his family history information.

Thanks to publishing director Nicola Legat for giving me this opportunity, and the team at Random House, including project manager Sam Hill and designer Trevor Newman, for making such a lovely book. And special thanks to Rob Shaw and Lucy Bennett, who had to cope with me surrounding myself with piles of books and writing madly at odd hours, right in the middle of our house.

Sarah Ell, Auckland, August 2008.

A NEW ZEALAND CHRISTMAS

Three centuries of Kiwi Christmas celebrations
from the Alexander Turnbull Library

Sarah Ell

GODWIT

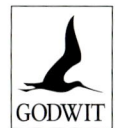

· Contents ·

6	Introduction	52	A partikilarly Happy Christmas ca 1900
		54	Remembrance flashed from land to land . . . ca 1900
8	*Metrosideros tomentosa* (pohutukawa) 1769	56	*A Native Pet* ca 1900
10	Mr & Mrs Chevalier send best wishes . . . ca 1860	58	NZ Christmas 1900s
12	*Shadows on the Snow: A Christmas Story* 1865	60	To greet you for a right happy Christmas 1900s
14	Church decorated for Christmas 1878	62	DIC Christmas flyer 1901
16	*Kainga of the Ladye Birds* 1879	64	Christmas greetings from the officers of the General Post Office 1901
18	Wairarapa Maori ca 1880s	66	*Auckland Weekly News* Christmas number 1902
20	Xmas Greetings from the Land of the Manuka 1880s	68	A merry Christmas 'Kia Ora' 1902
22	Wishing you a merry Christmas ca 1880s	70	*The House that Jack Built* 1903
24	'The Queen's Highway', or, How I spent Christmas morning 1881	72	A Merry Christmas & Happy New Year to us all 1903
26	Whitcombe & Tombs Ltd Christmas advertising price list 1884	74	Kia Ora, with the compliments of the Prime Minister 1905
28	Christmas and New Year Cards ca 1886	76	Compliments of the season ca 1905
30	The eruption of Tarawera and the destruction of the Pink and White Terraces ca 1886	78	Christmas in Fernland and at Home 1907
32	Grand Christmas performance of Handel's oratorio *The Messiah* 1889	80	Our hearts in Maoriland to-day . . . ca 1910
34	*Metrosideros tomentosa* (pohutukawa) 1890s	82	Christmas and New Year novelty cheques 1910s
36	A Merry Christmas to you ca 1891	84	Christmas Day menu, TSS *Ulimaroa* 1911
38	*A Southern Cross Fairy Tale* 1891	86	Christmas in the Far North of New Zealand 1912
40	*Some good old Christmas customs reversed by the female franchise* 1893	88	Letter to Father Christmas 1913
42	A memento of faithful service . . . 1893	90	Tables set for Christmas dinner, Maymorn camp 1915
44	*Ali Baba and the Forty Thieves* 1894	92	Christmas in a dug-out, Gallipoli 1915
46	The Stewart Island trip on board the *Wakatipu* 1895	94	Compliments of the season from France 1916
48	Compliments of the season from the Department of Lands and Survey 1896	96	Christmas menu, Sling Camp 1916
		98	A right loyal greeting 1916
50	Wishing Private Ross a Merry Christmas & a Happy New Year 1899	100	Dinner, Christmas Day, Ostrovo 1916
		102	The New Zealand Commander carves the turkey on Christmas Day 1917
		104	Hands across the sea 1917
		106	Cheerio from France 1918

108	Christmas greeting from New Zealand — ake ake 1914–18		160	Xmas 1944 1944
110	The 'digger' at Christmas 1917 and 1918		162	Greetings from 3 NZ General Hospital 1945
112	The Christmas spirit chases away gloom, malice and general selfishness 1919		164	Jayforce soldiers hosting a Christmas party for Japanese children 1946–48
114	*His Christmas dream* 1921		166	Sorting the Christmas mail at the General Post Office 1950
116	*The Sleeping Beauty* 1925		168	Christmas card from the New Zealand Legation, Paris 1950s
118	Nativity scene 1930s		170	Christmas turkeys in Korea 1951
120	Santa Claus promotes children's health camps 1931		172	Father Christmas goes to the Chatham Islands 1951
122	*First New Zealand Christmases* 1933		174	Scene at Tangiwai after the railway disaster 1953
124	Christmas shoppers' and gift givers' guide 1934		176	The Queen's Christmas at Government House 1953
126	He awhina — a friendly wish 1934		178	James Smith's Christmas corner 1955
128	Christmas and New Year holiday timetable 1934–35		180	Hutu and Kawa 1956–57
130	New Zealand tourist brochure ca 1935		182	*Tui or parson bird* 1957
132	*Santa Claus comes to Mussolini* 1935		184	With good wishes to you for Christmas and the New Year ca 1957
134	*Murphy's Moa and other Xmas sketches* 1936		186	Rumming the Christmas pudding, Campbell Island 1959
136	Christmas menus, Chateau Tongariro 1936 and 1937		188	Christmas menu, the Hermitage 1963
138	Attractions at the Evans Bay Xmas Carnival 1938		190	A Christmas season of *Casse-Noisette* 1963
140	Harry Walmsley's toy hospital 1938		192	'Behold I bring you good tidings of great joy' 1964
142	Victory 1942 calendar 1942		194	*Pohutukawa Carol* 1968
144	'Kia ora' from the No. 3 Section 6th Field Company 1941		196	Audience in the Majestic Theatre, Wellington 1968
146	Padre Holland at his altar, Christmas Day, Nofilia, Libya 1942		198	Save Manapouri 1970
148	Maori Battalion Christmas at Maadi Camp, Egypt 1943		200	Epiphany window design, Holy Trinity, Devonport 1974
150	Greetings from NZEF in the Pacific 1943		202	*Season of Peace and Goodwill* 1975
152	*Dossing Dulcie* 1943		204	Start of the school holidays 1977
154	Barbed Wire Happy Christmas Greetings ca 1943		206	Christmas Day in Auckland 1992
156	Christmas and New Year greetings from the New Zealand Engineers 1944			
158	Soldiers serving Christmas dinner at Faenza, Italy 1944		208	References

This page: Don Ramage, Eph-D-CABOT-Dance-1963-01 (p.190)
Opposite: Eileen Mayo, B-131-06-010 (p.84).

INTRODUCTION

The key purpose of the Alexander Turnbull Library is to preserve, protect, develop and make accessible the collections for all the people of New Zealand. *A New Zealand Christmas* is indeed a book that many New Zealanders will enjoy.

Starting with Sydney Parkinson's pohutukawa engraving from 1769 and concluding with Slane's Christmas cartoons from the early 1990s, Sarah Ell has collated a wonderful selection of items from the Turnbull collections spanning over three centuries. Images are drawn from across the library's various collecting formats, including drawings, paintings, prints, photographs, manuscripts, serials and books.

It is particularly pleasing to see so many items reproduced from the Turnbull's ephemera collections, an often overlooked resource containing a wealth of riches for researchers. In addition to numerous Yuletide postal greetings and Christmas cards, my favourites here include the 1911 Christmas Day menu from the trans-Tasman steamship *Ulimaroa*, and the programme from the 1879 pantomime production *Kainga of the Ladye Birds*.

Christmas in New Zealand was of course a colonial introduction, requiring some inventive adaptation. Pohutukawa blossoms and native fernery replaced holly and ivy as decorative symbols, and new Christmas stories and 'semi-Maori' pantomimes emerged. Later, New Zealanders' connections with British homelands were expressed through antipodean outpourings of Christmas cards and parcels, ensuring a golden age for the New Zealand postal service that extended well beyond the mid-twentieth century.

Photographs of New Zealanders during times of war are another feature: soldiers in a Gallipoli dug-out in 1915, nurses blowing the bugle for Christmas dinner in Serbia 1916, Maori Battalion soldiers preparing a hangi in Egypt 1943, and New Zealand troops happily handling huge turkeys in Korea, 1951. These are among the many vivid photographic images sourced from the Turnbull's photographic archive and published collections.

Alexander Turnbull bequeathed his library to the nation upon his death in 1918. Since opening its doors to the people of New Zealand in 1920, the library's collections have grown many times over. Today, the Turnbull, as part of the National Library of New Zealand, is the nation's pre-eminent research library. With over four million photographic images, manuscript collections measuring some nine kilometres, a hundred thousand drawings, paintings and prints, and over 350,000 books, the library is a rich research resource for all New Zealanders, or anyone with a research interest in New Zealand.

Most of the images in this book are now accessible online in digital form. More of the Turnbull collections will increasingly become available in this way over time. *A New Zealand Christmas* follows on from *Map New Zealand*, published in 2006. The Turnbull Library is very pleased to be working in partnership with Random House to publish featured highlights from the collections, together with informed commentary for a general audience.

The Turnbull is for all the people of New Zealand. Whether contained in a delicate early Hodgkins watercolour, or a more recent photograph of gleeful children escaping for the school holidays, the stories within the collections will resonate with New Zealanders in different ways, at different times, for different reasons. I trust *A New Zealand Christmas* will be enjoyed by many and be a welcoming introduction to the Alexander Turnbull Library.

Chris Szekely
Chief Librarian
Alexander Turnbull Library

1769 · Sydney Parkinson
Metrosideros tomentosa (pohutukawa)

The officers, scientists and seamen of Captain James Cook's *Endeavour* voyage were the first Europeans to observe and record the flowers of what would become known as New Zealand's Christmas tree, the pohutukawa.

Dutch explorer Abel Tasman had also been in New Zealand waters around Christmas, some 127 years earlier, in December 1642, but his ships were not on the lookout for botanical specimens. While they spent Christmas Day in Cook Strait, sailing away from what their captain had named Massacre Bay after the death of four crewmen in a skirmish with Maori, they did not make landfall or any mention of seeing bright red flowers. French explorer Jean de Surville was in Northland at the same time as Cook, but again, with crewmen sick with scurvy, the members of his expedition had other things on their minds.

This sketch of the flower, stem and buds of pohutukawa, then classified as *Metrosideros tomentosa* but now *M. excelsa*, is by young Scottish artist Sydney Parkinson, who was in his early 20s when he was employed for the *Endeavour* voyage by wealthy amateur botanist Joseph Banks. Parkinson made nearly 1000 drawings of plants, people and scenes as the *Endeavour* sailed through the Pacific to Tahiti, then southwest to New Zealand. Unfortunately he did not make it back to England, dying of dysentery on the way home in 1771.

While neither Parkinson nor Cook made mention in their journals of festivities aboard *Endeavour* on Christmas Day 1769, Banks noted:

> *Christmas day: Our Goose pye was eat with great approbation and in the Evening all hands were as Drunk as our forefathers usd to be upon the like occasion.*

This image is one of a series of black-and-white engravings of plant species made by Parkinson and used by Banks for his *Florilegium*, a catalogue of the species discovered on the journey which was finally published in 1988.

Parkinson, Sydney (1745–1771)
Botanical plates relating to Cook's first voyage.
Metrosideros tomentosa. *A. Rich. (Rata species). London, British Museum, 1890s.*
B-026-023

Metrosideros tomentosa A. Rich.

1860s · Nicholas Chevalier
Mr & Mrs Chevalier send best wishes for a Merry Christmas and happy New Year

Russian-born artist Nicholas Chevalier spent at least one Christmas in New Zealand in the 1860s, although it is not known whether this image of a festive picnic among the ferns represents a New Zealand or an Australian scene.

Chevalier trained as an artist in Switzerland, London and Italy before emigrating to Melbourne in 1854. He gained a reputation as a professional artist there through his work for the magazine *Melbourne Punch* and other commissioned work. While in Melbourne he married Caroline Wilkie, also an artist, and went on sketching trips around Victoria before sailing for Dunedin in November 1865. In New Zealand Chevalier was awarded £200 by the Otago Provincial Council to travel the province for three months, painting and drawing, in the hope that his artworks would be exhibited overseas and attract settlers to the booming colony. A few months later Canterbury province, not wanting to be outdone by its southern neighbour, did the same.

After travelling around Otago and Southland for several months, Chevalier was joined by Caroline in Christchurch. Together they travelled across the Southern Alps via the Hurunui Saddle and down the Taramakau Valley to Hokitika, returning via the largely unformed Arthur's Pass. Caroline Chevalier is believed to have been the first European woman to make the journey, and her account of it, held by the Alexander Turnbull Library, paints a vivid portrait of the rugged trip through the unexplored mountains.

The Chevaliers returned to Melbourne in August 1866, but Nicholas came back to New Zealand twice more: in November 1868, when he was caught up in fighting in Wanganui, and in April 1869, as a guide and artist with the Duke of Edinburgh. The couple then returned to London, where Nicholas continued to work as an artist until the 1890s.

Chevalier, Nicholas (1828–1902)
Mr & Mrs Chevalier send best wishes
 for a Merry Christmas and
 happy New Year [1860s?]
A-196-005

1865 • BENJAMIN LEOPOLD FARJEON
Shadows on the Snow: A Christmas Story

Published in Shadows on the snow, *by Benjamin L Farjeon*
B-K 843-FRONTIS

Shadows on the Snow was one of the first novels published in New Zealand, a Christmas story its author hoped would be welcomed 'as much from the kindly feeling engendered by the time, as from any merit of the work itself'.

Written by Benjamin Leopold Farjeon, it is the romantic and somewhat melodramatic story of a young Devonshire man who experiences a strange hallucination in the snow on Christmas Eve. Following a misunderstanding with his lover, he flees snowy England to the ends of the earth — or Otago, at least — where the misunderstanding is eventually resolved and the couple reunited.

In his preface to *Shadows*, Farjeon wrote:

It has long been a matter of surprise to [the author], that Christmas in this and other Colonies should have been so allowed to pass without some literary effort being made to recognise its genial influence. If the publication of this book serves as a link in the chain that binds the hearts of residents of the Colonies to their home-lands, his ambition will be satisfied.

Shadows on the Snow was the first New Zealand novel to use the Otago goldfields as a setting, after the precious metal had been discovered at Tuapeka in 1861. Farjeon had experience of the goldfields of Victoria, Australia, where he had set up several newspapers after emigrating from England in 1854. On arriving in New Zealand in 1861, he went into business with future prime minister Julius Vogel in the newly established *Otago Daily Times*.

Farjeon typeset *Shadows on the Snow* as he wrote it, and it was published by bookseller William Hay of Princes Street, Dunedin. The author sent a copy of the book to Charles Dickens, whose polite but noncommittal response seems to have inspired Farjeon to return to England and take up a full-time literary career. He became a successful and prolific novelist, producing more than 50 books. His daughter, Eleanor Farjeon, also became a well-known writer. Both *Shadows* and Farjeon's second novel, *Grif: A Story of Colonial Life* (1866), were illustrated by family friend Nicholas Chevalier (see page 10).

SHADOWS ON THE SNOW

A CHRISTMAS STORY

BY B. L. FARJEON

1878 · EAC Thomas
Church decorated for Christmas

The custom of decorating churches at Christmas was brought to New Zealand by the early European settlers, although in a country of unfamiliar plants and reversed seasons, local alternatives had to be found to the traditional holly and ivy.

The church shown here, probably St Thomas's in Motueka, is decorated with green boughs in the late Victorian tradition. The use of greenery as decoration in New Zealand was not in celebration of the abundant southern summer, but rather to continue the northern hemisphere tradition of brightening up what was essentially a midwinter festival. While some settlers did plant holly here, it didn't fruit at the right time, so nikau and fern fronds and the leaves of cabbage trees and flax were pressed into service as greenery. To add a touch of the traditional red, pohutukawa was used in the north, and rata, red roses or other cut flowers further south. Sometimes white flowers such as lilies were also added, as the new settlers tried to make themselves at home in their new land.

This image of a church decorated for Christmas comes from an album of photographs, many hand-coloured, and pencil and crayon sketches by EAC Thomas, who travelled to the Nelson area in late 1878 and spent around six months there. He stayed for some time with the Jones family of Motueka, then in March 1879 his party of about six, which from Thomas's paintings seems to have included at least one woman, travelled to the Mt Arthur tablelands inland of the town. Another photograph in the album shows the cottage of a Mrs Allan and family, Lower Moutere, who in November 1878, as the party made their way from Nelson to Motueka, 'took us in in a storm, dried our clothes, lent us a horse and gave us up the only fire the house had'.

Thomas, EAC, b 1825
Xmas. [ca 1879]
Hand-coloured photograph,
72 x 109 mm on sheet with watercolour
border additions 295 x 245 mm
E-305-q-003

1879
Kainga of the Ladye Birds

Kainga of the Ladye Birds or Harlequin Prince Tumanako, the Fair Ataahua and the Demon of Colonial Finance, described by writer, director and promoter RW Cary as 'a New Grand Semi-Maori Christmas pantomime', may be one of the great lost works of New Zealand theatre.

Performed for a short season at the Academy of Music, Wellington, at Christmas 1879, *Kainga of the Ladye Birds* brought together Maori legend, romance and political commentary, dancing ladybirds and 'a corps de ballet and army of cadets . . . courtiers, soldiers etc [and] a host of auxiliaries, the whole comprising no less than 75 performers'.

This programme includes the complete script of the show, which tells the tale of a love triangle between Ataahua ('the fair Puawai [blossom] of the Wharariki people', played by Miss Nell Gwynne), Maminga ('a fire worshipper from Tongariro', played by Miss Amy Thornton) and rival Whiro ('a fiery spirit from Taupo', played by Miss J Gwynne). It also takes pot shots at the state of the colonial economy with a subplot involving the Demon of Colonial Finance — who declares: 'You at once behold in me/New Zealand's greatest enemy/Finance I cripple, and credit limps' — and his 'satellite demons and his imps': Debenture, Taxation, Tariff, Ad. Valorem, Assessment and Per. Centage. The production owes much to Gilbert and Sullivan, with topical, contemporary references to Maori pacifist Te Whiti and Parihaka, investment in iron sand in Taranaki and local politicians Robert Stout, Julius Vogel and William Fox.

Cary, who also appeared in the pantomime in the dual roles of Pono, brother to Tumanako, 'Prince of Zealandia, and rear admiral of her Naval Forces', and Koura te Kino, Demon of Colonial Finance, was an actor and theatre impresario. Earlier in 1879 he had brought to New Zealand the first production of Gilbert and Sullivan's *The Pirates of Penzance*, just 18 months after its joint US and English premieres.

'Kainga of the Ladye Birds, or Harlequin Prince Tumanako, the fair ataahua, and The Demon of Colonial Finance. Fairy extravaganza opening to pantomime dialogue and songs written by 'Grif'. Produced by RW Cary.
Letterpress on programme cover, 163 x 100 mm.
Eph-A-PANTOMIME-1879-01-front

PRICE SIXPENCE.

ACADEMY OF MUSIC, WELLINGTON.

SOLE LESSEE - - - - - R. W. CARY.

FIRST TIME IN NEW ZEALAND.

A New Grand
SEMI-MAORI
CHRISTMAS PANTOMIME
ENTITLED
KAINGA OF THE LADYE BIRDS
OR
HARLEQUIN PRINCE TUMANAKO,
THE FAIR ATAAHUA,
AND
The Demon of Colonial Finance.

FOUNDED ON THE OLD NURSERY CHANT

"Ladye Bird, Ladye Bird, fly away home,
Your house is on fire, your children at home."

Fairy Extravaganza Opening to Pantomime Dialogue
and Songs written by
"GRIF."

The whole produced under the immediate direction of
R. W. CARY.

WELLINGTON:
PRINTED AT THE "N.Z. TIMES" OFFICE, WELLINGTON.

CA 1880S • THOMAS E PRICE
WAIRARAPA MAORI

This striking composite image of Wairarapa Maori from the 1880s makes an unusual Christmas card. It was compiled by Thomas E Price, a commercial photographer who ran a studio in Masterton during this period.

By the 1880s the Wairarapa had a population of around 6000 European settlers and a significant but increasingly landless Maori population. Masterton was the largest town, with a European population of around 3000. Price, who had earlier run a photographic studio in Timaru from 1875–78, was a prominent photographer in Masterton from 1879–1900. At other times he also ran studios at Taupo Quay in Wanganui, and in Tauranga and Waihi.

This image is held at the Alexander Turnbull Library as part of the collection of local historian Bennett Iorns, the great-grandson of Joseph Masters, one of the first settlers in the Wairarapa region, and after whom Masterton was named. The library also holds a number of other photographs by Price, many of Wairarapa Maori, including one labelled 'wife'.

This image is a cabinet photograph, a style of photographic print popular from the 1860s to the early twentieth century, mounted on card with the studio's name printed on it. It is a montage of head-and-shoulders portraits of Maori men and women, surrounded by Maori carvings and ferns, with an image of the meeting house at Te Ore Ore marae in the centre. Te Ore Ore is just to the east of Masterton and was the principal Maori settlement of the area at this time. The Ngati Hamua meeting house Nga Tau e Waru was built in the late 1870s but was destroyed by fire in 1939.

Composite photo by Thomas E Price of Wairarapa Maori, ca 1880s
Albumen print 104 x 150 mm on mount 108 x 166 mm, attached to album page
PA1-q-131-29

1880s • John Philemon Backhouse
Xmas Greetings from the Land of the Manuka

These beautiful greeting cards were painted by John Philemon Backhouse, a prolific artist who first came to New Zealand as a member of the corps of amateur soldiers offered grants of confiscated land in exchange for defending European-held territory during the New Zealand Wars.

Born in Ipswich, England, Backhouse arrived in Auckland in 1864, via Australia. He was initially stationed in Onehunga, where he married fellow immigrant Sarah Phillips before being sent to the fledgling military settlement of Hamilton. Once discharged from the Waikato Militia in 1866, he took up his land grant and set up business as a house and carriage painter.

Although based in Hamilton, Backhouse travelled widely around New Zealand and made several trips to Australia. He visited and painted the thermal region of Rotorua in the early 1880s, before the eruption of Mount Tarawera and the destruction of the Pink and White Terraces (see page 30). After separating from his wife around 1900, he moved to Wairoa on the East Coast, where he painted and taught art until his death in 1908.

As well as drawing and painting for his own pleasure, Backhouse produced cards and shell paintings of New Zealand scenes for the tourist market. The two images seen here fall into this category: one, inscribed 'Xmas Greetings from the Land of the Manuka', shows a lake edged with flowering pohutukawa, inset into a spray of manuka and maidenhair fern; the other, 'For Auld Lang Syne', shows a rewarewa flower and a waterfall.

Backhouse also painted birds and insects, and more than 270 of his paintings and sketches of New Zealand and Australian subjects from the 1870s and 1880s are held by the Alexander Turnbull Library. Much of the collection the library holds today was acquired by Turnbull himself, probably during Backhouse's lifetime.

Backhouse, John Philemon (1845–1908)
Christmas card with manuka and lake scene, ca 1880 and New Year card with rewarewa and waterfall, ca 1880
Oil on page 183 x 203 mm
E-053-020 and E-053-021

1880s • Isabel Hodgkins
Wishing you a merry Christmas

This Christmas watercolour is by Isabel Hodgkins (later Field), a member of one of New Zealand's best-known artistic families. She was the elder sister of Frances Hodgkins and the daughter of William Mathew Hodgkins.

While Frances (see page 36) eventually became the better-known artist, initially Isabel was considered to show greater promise. The sisters were both privately educated and encouraged in artistic pursuits by their father, a central figure in Dunedin's burgeoning arts scene (see page 46). Even in her teens, Isabel was a talented landscape painter and watercolourist, also painting flowers and still lifes, and she was elected to membership of the Otago Art Society at the age of 16. By 1888 she had made enough money from the sale of her artwork to take an extended holiday in Australia. Despite the suggestion of a marriage proposal in Melbourne, at this stage she considered herself a confirmed spinster — even though she was only 21.

Everything changed in 1891, however, when she met young lawyer William Hughes Field while on a trip to Wellington. They were engaged after just a few months and married in April 1893. The couple moved to Wellington, and Isabel continued to paint in the early years of her marriage. However, after Field was elected to Parliament in 1900, and with four children and a busy social schedule, Isabel's life took a very different direction to that of her sister.

These images are part of an album of sketches by members of the Hodgkins family dating from the 1880s, including works by Isabel, Mary, William and family friend May Kenyon. It also includes photographs of Isabel and her husband, with one of their children as a baby.

Hodgkins, Isabel Jane (1867–1950)
Wishing you a merry Christmas
Watercolour, 102 x 157 mm on album page,
259 x 161 mm
E-311-q-018-1

1881 • Harold Bullock-Webster
'The Queen's Highway', or, How I spent Christmas morning 1881

Few New Zealanders today would rely on public transport to get to their destination on Christmas Day. The situation was not so different in the 1880s, as new immigrant Harold Bullock-Webster found out, to his detriment.

Bullock-Webster, Harold (1855–1942)
'The Queen's Highway', or, How I spent Christmas morning 1881, by Harry Bullock-Webster; dedicated to Miss Williamson.
Dec. 26th, 1881
Booklet containing 6 ink and watercolour sketches 110 x 78 mm
E-408-q

Bullock-Webster made this series of sketches on Boxing Day to illustrate his adventures of the day before, when trying to catch an omnibus — which at that time would have been horse-drawn — back from a tennis match. He had not long been in Auckland nor in New Zealand at this time, so could perhaps be forgiven for not appreciating the vagaries of the public transport service.

Born in England in 1855, Bullock-Webster went to Canada in his late teens as a cadet with the Hudson's Bay Company, a massive trading enterprise that had been the first commercial venture established in North America. While on leave in England, he met one of New Zealand's best-known businessmen and land speculators, Thomas Russell, who had returned to London to run his colonial affairs at a distance. He offered Bullock-Webster a position inspecting his various estates and interests in New Zealand, as his current agent was not up to travelling around the 'rather . . . rough and roadless country'.

Bullock-Webster arrived in Christchurch in 1881 to report on several properties, then moved on to the Waikato and Auckland. There he met James Williamson, another businessman and speculator who had bought Russell's property in Hillsborough, Pah Farm, and built Auckland's grandest home, The Pah (now Monte Cecilia House). Williamson invited Bullock-Webster to spend Christmas 1881 with the family, whereupon he met Williamson's daughter Maud, to whom this series of sketches is dedicated. 'It did not take me long to fall in love with this daughter of the house,' he wrote in his lively, self-illustrated autobiography, *From the Hudson's Bay Company to New Zealand*, published in 1938.

The pair were married several years later and settled in Hamilton, where Bullock-Webster set up the Waikato Hunt Club. Later, after moving to Auckland, he became Master of the Pakuranga Hounds.

1884 • WHITCOMBE & TOMBS LTD CHRISTMAS ADVERTISING PRICE LIST

A toga-clad woman in a seashell chariot drawn by children of all nations, beneath a banner suspended by classical angels, bedecked the Christmas catalogue from the fledgling company Whitcombe & Tombs in 1884.

Whitcombe & Tombs, the predecessor of today's Whitcoulls book and stationery stores, was established in Christchurch in the late 1870s. The original firm was set up by George Whitcombe, the son of an English army captain, who came to New Zealand in 1871 to join his brother Charles who was serving with British troops here. After a brief period in the Armed Constabulary George Whitcombe moved to Christchurch and set up a bookselling and stationery business, before joining forces with Christchurch printer, binder and lithographer George Tombs in late 1882. Whitcombe & Tombs was one of the first companies registered in New Zealand under the Companies Act.

Originally a printer and book publisher as well as a retailer, the company specialised in publishing books for the educational market, taking advantage of the introduction of compulsory primary schooling in 1877. It grew quickly, with branches established in Dunedin, Wellington and London. Following Whitcombe's death in 1917 the company was taken over by his son Bertie, a popular and colourful character who ran it as very much a family business until his death in 1965. The name was changed to Whitcoulls when the company merged with printers and stationers Coulls, Somerville, Wilkie in 1971.

This price list for 1884 shows that the range of goods stocked by Whitcombe & Tombs was similar to today, with an emphasis on books and stationery. It draws particular attention to the selection of cards, including AD Willis's chromolithographed cards of New Zealand subjects (see pages 28 and 30), plush folding cards, and leather-worked, ivory, porcelain and 'terracottine' cards. These were to be 'arranged on long tables, with a distinct staff of assistants, so that a large number can select at one time without inconvenience'.

Whitcombe and Tombs Limited, Cashel St, Christchurch. Whitcombe & Tombs Limited, lith. [Front cover. 1884] Lithograph, brown and cream on white paper, 278 x 222 mm
Eph-B-BOOKSELLER-1884-01-front

ca 1886 • AD Willis
Christmas and New Year cards

By the 1880s, images of New Zealand's stunning natural scenery and growing townships had become popular subjects for Christmas cards being sent back 'Home'. These two, and those on page 32, were produced by Wanganui firm AD Willis.

Printer Archibald Duddington Willis came to New Zealand in 1857 and worked in various parts of the country, including the Otago goldfields, before settling in Wanganui in 1867. Here he set up the *Wanganui Herald* with John Ballance, founder of the New Zealand Liberal Party and later the country's premier. Willis then expanded into commercial printing, bookbinding and publishing, as well as the sale of books and stationery.

Around 1886 AD Willis produced a series of 66 chromolithographed cards, of which the Alexander Turnbull Library holds a sample book. A note from the donor, Robert Coupland Harding, states: 'Most, if not all, of the floral studies were designed and drawn by my cousin, Miss Lydia Harding of Whanganui, now (1911) Mrs Swain, of Waipawa, Hawke's Bay'. The cards, which come in two main sizes (around 70 mm x 100 mm and 100 mm x 145 mm) show landscapes from around New Zealand, often paired with native plants and flowers, images of cities and towns, and scenes of Maori life. At the turn of the century, the *Cyclopedia of New Zealand* described Willis's well-known cards as being 'intended . . . to afford some idea of the almost unlimited variety of scenery which is so attractive a characteristic of the Colony'.

These two show the peaceful beauty of Lake Wakatipu — somewhat improbably paired with subtropical nikau palms — and the industrial landscape of Grahamstown. The latter was one of two goldmining settlements that became the town of Thames, and was characterised by the stamper batteries used to pound gold from quartz deposits found near the town. By 1886 the field was in decline, and it closed down in the 1920s.

Willis, Archibald Duddington (Firm) Nikau Palm, N.Z. A merry Christmas and Grahamstown goldfield, Thames, N.Z. A bright New Year; Wanganui; A.D. Willis, [ca 1886].
Chromolithograph 145 x 104 mm on album page ca 137 x 180 mm and chromolithograph 104 x 72 mm on album page ca 137 x 180 mm
E-068-018 and E-068-017-2

CA 1886 · AD WILLIS
THE ERUPTION OF TARAWERA AND THE DESTRUCTION OF THE PINK AND WHITE TERRACES

In 1886, the sudden eruption of Mount Tarawera near Rotorua provided rich fodder for Christmas card printer AD Willis (see page 28). The company dedicated five cards to images of the eruption and the lost Pink and White Terraces.

T he terraces, on the shores of Lake Rotomahana at the foot of Mount Tarawera, were a major tourist attraction touted as 'the eighth wonder of the world'. The White Terraces were the larger, around 3 ha in area, 30 m high and 240 m long, fronting onto Lake Rotomahana. The Pink Terraces, about 1.5 km away across the lake, were smaller and lower, but considered superior for bathing. Both were utterly destroyed in the cataclysmic eruption of June 10, 1886, in which at least 108 people were smothered and died (some put the figure as high as 153) and a large swathe of the Rotorua district was covered in a blanket of ash.

The upper card — somewhat incongruously wishing the recipient a joyous Christmas — features the fabled White Terraces. The two views show the lost terraces and their spectacular blue pools close up, from the front, and in a wider view from the side, backed with sprays of pohutukawa buds and flowers, probably painted by Lydia Harding (see page 28).

The 'Happy New Year' card features a circular vignette of the mountain erupting and the ash-covered remains of a mill, surrounded by unidentified white berries. The central image of the volcano exploding while figures at the Maori village in the foreground look on in anguish was based on a painting by Charles Blomfield, who painted some of the best-known images of the terraces before their destruction. Blomfield did not witness the eruption, so the image is a reconstruction. However, both Charles and his nephew, fellow artist William Blomfield (see page 40), visited the scene shortly after the event.

Willis, Archibald Duddington (Firm) White Terraces destroyed by eruption 1886. A joyous Christmas; and Tarawera eruption, N.Z. 1886. A Happy New Year. Wanganui; A.D. Willis, [ca 1886] Chromolithograph 105 x 144 mm on album page ca 137 x 180 mm and chromolithograph 72 x 104 mm on album page ca 137 x 180 mm E-068-003 and E-068-006-1

1889 • Christchurch Musical Society Grand Christmas Performance of Handel's Oratorio *The Messiah*

Performances of George Handel's *Messiah* have long been a tradition at Christmas — even if the oratorio was originally written to be performed during Lent. The work was performed by a local choral society in Auckland as early as 1856, and by the 1890s it was a regular and popular Christmastime event in many cities.

This performance, by the Christchurch Musical Society, featured a programme of readings and recitations by members of the society's committee, as well as combined voices of the Liedertafel male choir, the Motett Societies, 'and all the leading choirs in Christchurch and the neighbourhood'. The 'festival chorus and orchestra' were conducted by FM Wallace, a music teacher who was one of the pioneers of the Canterbury music scene and a founding member of the Canterbury Society of Musicians. At the time of this performance, the society's secretary and treasurer was architect Samuel Hurst Seagar, who helped to design the Canterbury University College buildings, as well as many grand homes around Christchurch in the Arts and Crafts style.

The performance was held at the Palace skating rink, between Armagh and Gloucester streets, which later became the Colosseum movie theatre. As well as this performance of *Messiah* (the correct title has no 'the') on December 19 and on Christmas night, the rink was hosting the Canterbury Grand National Baby Show, offering £100 in prizes.

The Christchurch Musical Society was established in 1860 as the Canterbury Vocal Union, then combined with the St Cecilia Society to form a mixed choir. In 1920 it added 'Royal' to its name. It was the oldest continually operating choral group in New Zealand until it merged with the Christchurch Harmonic Society to become the Christchurch City Choir in 1991.

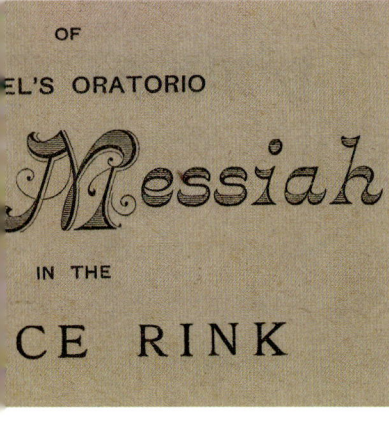

Christmas Musical Society Grand Christmas performance of Handel's oratoria 'The Messiah' in the Palace Rink by the Christchurch Musical Society, assisted by members of the Liedertafel, Motett Societies, and all the leading choirs in Christchurch and the neighbourhood. Thursday, December 19, 1889.
[Front cover, 1889]
Letterpress on pale pink front cover, 203 x 133 mm.
Eph-A-MUSIC-1889-02-front

CHRISTCHURCH MUSICAL SOCIETY

Grand Christmas Performance

OF

HANDEL'S ORATORIO

"The Messiah"

IN THE

PALACE RINK

BY THE

CHRISTCHURCH MUSICAL SOCIETY

ASSISTED BY THE MEMBERS OF THE LIEDERTAFEL, MOTETT SOCIETIES, AND ALL THE LEADING CHOIRS IN CHRISTCHURCH AND THE NEIGHBOURHOOD.

THURSDAY, DECEMBER 19TH, 1889

FESTIVAL CHORUS AND ORCHESTRA

UNDER THE CONDUCTORSHIP OF MR. F. M. WALLACE

SOLOISTS:

Soprano—Mrs. Garrard.   *Contralto*—Mrs. Wilson.

Tenor—Mr. A. Appleby.   *Bass*—Mr. M. A. Millar.

ORGANIST: MR. NORMINGTON.   LEADER: MR. SKELTON.   CONDUCTOR: MR. F. M. WALLACE.

Whitcombe & Tombs Limited, Stationers and Printers, Christchurch.   14761

1890s • Emily Cumming Harris
Metrosideros tomentosa (pohutukawa)

More than 200 years after Sydney Parkinson's representation of the New Zealand Christmas tree (see page 9), this image was made by Emily Harris. Harris is now thought of as one of New Zealand's most successful female botanical artists, yet she suffered persistent anxiety about her life and work.

Harris, whose diaries and correspondence as well as many of her paintings are held by the Alexander Turnbull Library, emigrated to New Zealand as a child. Her family was among the passengers on the *William Bryan*, the first organised immigrant ship to arrive in New Plymouth, in March 1841. Harris's father Edwin was an amateur artist as well as being a civil engineer and surveyor. When hostilities broke out in Taranaki in 1860, Emily was sent to Hobart to study art, while the rest of the family was evacuated to Nelson.

From the 1870s, Harris and her sisters, none of whom ever married, ran a small private school in Nelson. Much of her time was taken up with teaching and running the household after the death of her mother in 1879, but she persisted with her painting despite her continuing worries about its quality. The family held several exhibitions in Nelson and New Plymouth, and Harris supplemented the household income by selling her work. She won many awards and also exhibited internationally, in Melbourne and London. Living the financially precarious life of an independent woman, Harris continued to paint until her death in 1925.

Three volumes of lithographs of Harris's botanical drawings were published in 1890: *New Zealand Flowers*, *New Zealand Ferns* and *New Zealand Berries*. This painting comes from a later, unpublished series of watercolours, entitled *New Zealand flowers in colour, Volume 3*. The Alexander Turnbull Library acquired 63 of Harris's watercolours in 1924 for 10 shillings each.

Harris, Emily Cumming (1837?–1925)
Metrosideros tomentosa (pohutukawa)
[1890s?]
Watercolour
B-018-010

Metrosideros tomentosa
(pohutukawa)

ca 1891 • Frances Hodgkins
A Merry Christmas to you

This delicate watercolour wishing the viewer a merry Christmas gives little indication of the later painting style that would make Frances Hodgkins one of New Zealand's best-known artists.

Hodgkins was still in her early 20s when she painted this image, which forms the centrepiece of a montage in a family scrapbook that also features works by her sister Isabel (see page 22) and father William (see page 46).

Frances Hodgkins was a late starter compared with Isabel, who was originally considered 'the artist' of the two sisters while Frances was steered towards musical studies. However, by the early 1890s Frances had begun to take her painting more seriously, joining the Otago Art Society as a working member and showing her work in Dunedin and Christchurch. Her early pictures were often portraits of her family and their domestic staff. She began to study under immigrant Italian artist Girolamo Nerli and enrolled at the Dunedin School of Art, both to study the discipline of art and to train as a teacher.

Following her father's death in 1898, Frances went to England to study, paint and travel, often in the company of fellow artist Dorothy Kate Richmond. In 1903 she became the first New Zealand artist to be hung 'on the line' at the Royal Academy of Arts in London, before returning to her native country to teach and continue to paint and exhibit.

She returned to Europe in 1906 and spent much of the rest of her life there, travelling widely and building a reputation as one of the foremost artists of her time, developing a distinctive modernist style that was far removed from her early watercolours. She died in England in 1947, shortly before being nominated for a CBE by the British prime minister.

Hodgkins, Frances Mary (1869–1947)
A Merry Christmas to you [Girl's head.
ca 1891]
Watercolour 140 x 105 mm
E-312-q-046-5

1891 • KATE McCOSH CLARK
A SOUTHERN CROSS FAIRY TALE

This children's book by Kate McCosh Clark, written in New Zealand but published in London, attempted to explain to English readers what a New Zealand Christmas was like.

The book tells the story of two children, Hal and Cis, who are taken on a magical journey around New Zealand on Christmas Eve by a youthful Santa Claus. McCosh Clark wanted the book to inform as well as entertain; it contains notes on birds by naturalist Andreas Reischek, and information on geology by geologist Algernon Thomas. The cover engraving shows the children and sprightly Santa standing on what appears to be the recently destroyed Pink and White Terraces at Tarawera (see page 30). The illustrations were by Clark and Robert Atkinson, a British artist who had a studio in Auckland's Victoria Arcade. McCosh Clark wrote in her introduction:

> *There are, growing up under the Southern Cross, generations of children with English speech and English hearts, to whom the Yule-log at Christmas is un-meaning and the snow unknown. The little story which follows is written for such children as these, and also for those in the older land who have any desire to know what Christmas is like among their kin on the other side of the world.*

Little is known of McCosh Clark's early life, but she was born Kate Woolnough in Ipswich, England in 1847, and worked as a researcher for writers before emigrating to Melbourne, Australia. There she met and married wealthy New Zealand businessman James McCosh Clark, 14 years her senior, who had made his money through investment in the Thames goldfields. James McCosh Clark was mayor of Auckland from 1880 to 1883 and established the city's first public library. As mayoress, Kate had an active social and public life, was a patron of music and other arts, and helped to re-form the Auckland Society of Arts. However, after some bad financial decisions and business failures the McCosh Clarks fell from grace and they returned to England in 1889, where Kate pursued her career as a writer. She returned to New Zealand after her husband's death and died in Auckland in 1926.

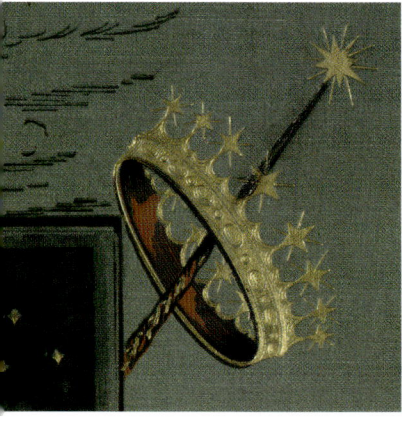

Published in A Southern Cross fairy tale *by Kate McCosh Clark; with illustrations by R. Atkinson and the author (London: Sampson Low, Marston, Searle & Rivington, 1891)*
B-K 448-COVER, P J823

1893 · WILLIAM BLOMFIELD
SOME GOOD OLD CHRISTMAS CUSTOMS REVERSED BY THE FEMALE FRANCHISE

At Christmas 1893, New Zealand was abuzz with reaction to women being granted the right to vote in local body and parliamentary elections. Here, artist and political cartoonist William Blomfield takes a satirical look at the reversal of the sexes that many people feared would result from giving women the right to vote.

New Zealand was the first country in the world to confer the right to vote on all adult women, after nearly 10 years of agitation and much opposition and political manoeuvring. Women could not stand for Parliament until 1919, however, and the first female Member of Parliament, Mabel Howard, was not elected until 1933. But in November 1893 Elizabeth Yates was elected mayor of Onehunga — the first female mayor in the British Empire.

At this time women were viewed as the moral guardians of society, and many of those opposed to granting them the right to vote believed it would cause the breakdown of society. Blomfield's cartoon suggests some role-reversals that might occur with a female 'head of the household', including a woman suggesting to her children, 'You must all praise the pudding. Your papa has worked hard all morning to make a nice Christmas dinner, and you must show him how pleased you are.'

William Blomfield was the nephew of prominent colonial artist Charles Blomfield. He worked as an artist for *The New Zealand Herald*, sketching current events in the days before news photography. One of his more interesting assignments was to visit Mount Tarawera shortly after the eruption, to investigate whether the Pink and White Terraces had in fact been destroyed (see page 30). He started work as an artist and cartoonist for the weekly tabloid *New Zealand Observer and Free Lance* in 1887, and worked for its various iterations for 51 years, every week drawing the full-page cover cartoon as well as many illustrations for the interior.

Blomfield, William (1866–1938)
Some good old Christmas customs reversed by the female franchise, New Zealand Observer and Free Lance, *23 December 1893*
A4 size photocopy
H-713-061

SOME GOOD OLD CHRISTMAS CUSTOMS REVERSED BY THE FEMALE FRANCHISE.

1893
A MEMENTO OF FAITHFUL SERVICE . . .

Liberal politician Fred Pirani had a lot to thank his constituents for at Christmas 1893, after he was voted into Parliament for the first time as the MP for Palmerston North. Pirani was the Liberal candidate for the electorate as the party swept to victory in the November elections under the leadership of Richard 'King Dick' Seddon.

Seddon had taken the reins of the left-wing Liberal party in April 1893, after the death of premier John Ballance, and amid concerns about the effect of women voting for the first time, the Liberals secured a handy victory. This card shows that Pirani's seat anyway was secure, highlighting his election-day margins over his nearest rival, Conservative candidate GM Sheldon, and JP Leary (standing as an independent).

Pirani was an Australian-born printer and journalist who came to New Zealand with his parents when he was six. He settled in Palmerston North in 1884 and became active in local politics, especially relating to education. He stood for Parliament unsuccessfully in 1890, representing the local branch of the international Knights of Labor and losing by 61 votes, but was named as the Liberal candidate by Seddon in 1893. He soon fell out with Seddon, however, and tried to establish a breakaway party before the 1896 election. Seddon endorsed a different candidate for Palmerston North in 1900, and although Pirani held onto his seat he was forced to retire due to ill health in 1902. He stood for Parliament three more times but was never re-elected.

The second caricature on the paper, by an unknown artist, is of William Pember Reeves, one of Pirani's Liberal colleagues. Also a former journalist and one-time lawyer, Reeves was first elected to Parliament in 1887, in opposition. He became an active member of Ballance's Liberal Party but he too clashed with Seddon, and in 1896 he departed for London to be New Zealand's agent general and later high commissioner.

Christmas greeting card from Fred Pirani and two sketches Dec 1893
Green and red greeting card 103 mm x 165 mm with oval sepia photograph, one pencil sketch and an ink and pencil sketch
qMS-1382-032

New Zealand General Election, 1893.

PALMERSTON SEAT:
- FRED. PIRANI, Liberal 1,754
- G. M. SNELSON, Conservative .. 1,551
- J. P. LEARY, Independent .. 400

WITH THE COMPLIMENTS OF THE SEASON·

A MEMENTO OF FAITHFUL SERVICE FROM YOU·

Yours right truly,

Fred Pirani

Palmerston North.

December, 1893.

Reeves

Pirani

1894
Pollard's Lilliputian Opera Company
Ali Baba and the Forty Thieves

Pollard's Lilliputian Opera Company was one of the more unusual theatrical troupes that regularly toured New Zealand in the 1880s and 1890s, and its Christmas season of *Ali Baba* in 1894 was a popular production.

The company was established by James Pollard, an English-born piano tuner who emigrated to Australia in 1860 and set up a troupe of child entertainers, drawing mainly on members of his own family. All 15 of his children appeared in its first production, in 1880, a juvenile version of Gilbert and Sullivan's *HMS Pinafore*. The show was such a success in Pollard's hometown of Launceston, Tasmania, that it was taken on tour to New Zealand, where it played to packed houses, before touring throughout Australia, Singapore and India. Pollard died at the end of this first tour and the company was taken over by Thomas O'Sullivan, a member of the original troupe who married one of Pollard's daughters and adopted her surname.

In 1894 the company toured New Zealand with *Ali Baba and the Forty Thieves*, on the heels of its success the previous year with *The Gondoliers, Aladdin* and *The Pirates of Penzance*. A notice in the *Evening Post* described the first night of the show as 'an unparalled success, achieved by the People's Favourites', with the theatre 'packed from floor to ceiling, people hanging on to the fresco work. Inside a sea of smiling faces; outside, sorrowing and disappointed hundreds' — no doubt with a touch of hyperbole.

Unfortunately, tragedy struck when the show reached Palmerston North in March 1895. After a rapturously received opening night at the Theatre Royal, the company awoke the next day to discover the venue had burned to the ground, destroying all their scenery, props and costumes, none of which was insured. However, public sympathy and donations soon saw the company back on its feet, putting on a hastily prepared production of *Uncle Tom's Cabin*.

Grand Opera House (Wellington); Pollard's Lilliputian Opera Company in the new grand Christmas pantomime, 'Ali Baba and the Forty Thieves'. Boxing Day, Wed[nesday] 26 [Programme. 1894]. Programme of 29 pages, 215 x 135 mm
Eph-A-PANTOMIME-1894-01

The TROCADERO
WILLIS STREET, WELLINGTON.

Best appointed Dining-rooms in the Colony. All visitors to Wellington patronise the TROCADERO. Private entrance to the Ladies' Dining-room.

POLLARD'S LILIPUTIAN OPERA COMPANY

In the New Grand Christmas Pantomime,

[MR. TOM POLLARD, Sole Lessee and Proprietor.]

Ali Baba and the Forty Thieves

THE * TROCADERO
WELLINGTON. WILLIS STREET. WELLINGTON.

Private Dinners, Suppers, and Banquets a Speciality. All leading citizens patronise the TROCADERO.
Cuisine unsurpassed. Cleanliness, Civility, Attention.

Printed at Evening Post Office, Willis Street.

1895 · William Mathew Hodgkins
The Stewart Island trip on board the Wakatipu

Few people today would plan to go on a trip on Christmas Day itself, but in the late nineteenth century, Christmas and Boxing days and two days at New Year were the only major holidays most workers received.

20

Dunedin-based artist and lawyer William Mathew Hodgkins probably had the luxury of more extended holidays when he made this trip to Stewart Island, but many of the other passengers were probably making the most of the two days off to have an 'excursion'. While Christmas Day had always been considered a holiday in New Zealand, Boxing Day was regarded as being mostly an English holiday and did not become widely accepted until the early twentieth century.

This drawing is one of a series in a sketchbook made by Hodgkins on a few days' holiday to Stewart Island between Christmas 1895 and New Year 1896. Other watercolours from the trip show scenes at sea during the crossing of Foveaux Strait and at Halfmoon Bay. There is no evidence that he was accompanied on the trip by either of his artistic daughters, Isabel (see page 22) and Frances (see page 36).

Hodgkins, who primarily painted landscapes, was an inveterate traveller, and toured the country in pursuit of artistic subjects despite financial difficulties. He was declared bankrupt in 1888, and the family lived a life of genteel penury. His health declined during the 1890s and he died in 1898, leaving his family in debt.

The SS *Wakatipu* on which Hodgkins travelled to Stewart Island seems to have been a somewhat unlucky ship: it ran aground in the Victoria Channel between Port Chalmers and Dunedin, and in 1898 collided with and sank the sailing ship *Laira* at the Dunedin wharves.

William Mathew Hodgkins (1833–1898)
The Stewart Island trip on board the
Wakatipu, Christmas day, 1895
Watercolour 170 x 255 mm
A-182-001

1896
COMPLIMENTS OF THE SEASON FROM THE DEPARTMENT OF LANDS AND SURVEY

This Christmas card from the Department of Lands and Survey was in a way sent from father to son — from Surveyor-General Stephenson Percy Smith to his son Maurice Crompton Smith, at this time working in the department's Wellington district office.

As a cadet, Maurice Smith was one of the first men to survey the Urewera when it was still under Tuhoe control, and he was later responsible for the laying out of roads in the Tokaanu and Tongariro areas. As well as also working in the Wellington and Taranaki areas, he was acting surveyor-general in 1922 and was a foundation member of the New Zealand Institute of Surveyors, which still awards a prize in his name each year. His father, S. Percy Smith, was one of New Zealand's first professional surveyors, who also wrote widely on ethnological subjects.

The 1890s were a busy time for the newly formed Department of Lands and Survey, with the Liberal government pushing ahead with its land-reform laws. The Liberals, led by Richard Seddon, were keen to make more land available for settlement, so they introduced new land taxes that aimed to discourage large holdings and absentee landlords, and purchased large estates to break them up into smaller farms available for lease. Between 1892 and 1911 the government divided up more than 200 estates into nearly 5000 small farms, making 3.5 million hectares of land available for settlement — and needing to be surveyed.

Early surveys of land and records of land ownership in New Zealand were kept in a rather haphazard way by officials in the various provinces, until the Department of the Surveyor-General was created in 1876, merging with the Crown Lands Department in 1891 to form the Department of Lands and Survey. The department was responsible for surveying and administering lands (including Maori land), maintaining all land-title survey plans and records, producing maps and administering public reserves and domains. It was restructured and its functions broken up in 1987.

NZ Lands and Survey Department
The compliments of the season to Mr MC Smith, from the Department of Lands and Survey, Wellington, NZ. Christmas, 1896
Greeting card, 190 x 230 mm
A-174-001

1899
WISHING PRIVATE ROSS A MERRY CHRISTMAS & A HAPPY NEW YEAR

At Christmas 1899, for the first time in our history, New Zealand troops were overseas on active service — and they each received a Christmas card from the premier, Richard Seddon, to commemorate the festive season.

The contingent of soldiers who left Wellington in October 1899 for what became known as the Boer War was the first New Zealand unit to fight in an overseas war. Around 40,000 people — about five per cent of New Zealand's entire population at the time — turned out to watch their departure for what became a somewhat inglorious conflict.

This was actually the second Boer War; British interests in South Africa and the Boers (now known as Afrikaners) had been in conflict for more than 50 years and hostilities had previously broken out in 1880. The British had been soundly defeated in the Transvaal in 1881, and resentments simmered. The discovery of gold in the region in 1886 caused tensions to rise again, resulting in the outbreak of war in October 1889.

Seddon led the House of Representatives to approve sending a force of around 200 mounted riflemen to support Mother England, and New Zealand was swept up in patriotic fervour. As well as the country's small permanent armed forces, the government called for volunteers, and more than 500 men came forward within a few days. The volunteers converged at Wellington, where they were given basic training at a camp established on a farm at Karori before being farewelled with massive fanfare, departing on the SS *Waiwera* for Cape Town. The inside of this eight-page booklet card has photographs of the troops gathering and departing.

While many people expected the conflict to be quickly resolved, in fact it dragged on for three years, with the Imperial troops struggling to combat the Boers' guerrilla tactics. Ten New Zealand contingents, totalling around 6500 men, were sent to South Africa, where 97 soldiers were killed in action or died in accidents and a further 133 died of disease.

With the Premier's compliments; wishing [Pte Ross] a Merry Christmas & a Happy New Year, Decr 1899. [Signed] R Seddon. Govt Printing Office, 1899 [Cover]. Photolithograph on cover of booklet of 8 pages, 145 x 220 mm
Eph-A-CARDS-Christmas-Seddon-1899-cover

Robley, Horatio Gordon 1840–1930
A partikilarly Happy Xmas [ca 1900?]
Ink & watercolour over pencil 309 x 246 mm (irreg)
E-450-q-003

CA 1900 · HG ROBLEY
A PARTIKILARLY HAPPY XMAS

Soldier-artist Horatio Robley spent only a couple of years in New Zealand, mostly in the Bay of Plenty, but the Maori customs he observed had a lifelong effect. This Christmas card from the early 1900s, 30 years after he had served in New Zealand, shows he retained his interest in Maori art and culture.

23

Robley was a British army officer who came to New Zealand with the 68th Durham Light Regiment in 1864. He had already served in Burma, where he had become interested in and sketched local art and artefacts. He continued his role as a 'soldier with a pencil' once stationed in New Zealand, buying a Maori dictionary and several books about Maori culture before being sent to Tauranga in April 1864. On April 28 he fought in what became known as the Battle of Gate Pa, entering the abandoned pa the next day and making drawings that were reproduced in the *Illustrated London News* in June 1864 — the first images of the war to be seen by the British public.

Robley travelled around the Bay of Plenty during the time he was stationed there, going as far east as Opotiki in pursuit of the Hauhau rebels who had killed missionary Carl Volkner. Robley studiously recorded Maori carving and tattoo patterns and his drawings were also used to military advantage: a sketch he had made of Gate Pa while on a duck-shooting and sketching expedition was used to plan the attack on the fortification.

Robley's regiment returned to Britain in 1866, and in the 1880s he was promoted to the rank of major and sent to Africa. He retired as a major general in 1887, when stationed in Ceylon (now Sri Lanka). In his retirement he continued to draw and pursue his interest in Maori art and tattoo. He published two books, on moko and on greenstone, and frequently decorated his correspondence with Maori designs.

As well as this punful Christmas drawing, the Alexander Turnbull Library also holds drafts of several other cards using Maori words and drawings; one wishes the recipient a 'mere' Christmas.

a partikilarly Happy Xmas — HGR

24

ca 1900
Remembrance flashed from land to land …

For many New Zealanders around the turn of the century, Christmas was a time for gathering together the immediate family while extended family celebrated a very different Christmas on the other side of the world.

However, the introduction and spread of wireless telegraphy made 'Home' seem a little less far away. The first commercially viable telegraph system was developed in England in the 1830s, and the first local public system set up between Christchurch and Lyttelton in the early 1860s. The technology spread rapidly, often hand in hand with the growth of railways.

New Zealand was linked to New South Wales by undersea cable in 1876, and thus indirectly to the United Kingdom via Adelaide, Darwin, Java, India and stations in the Mediterranean. It wasn't until 1902 that it became more directly linked to the wider world through the laying of the Pacific Cable. This provided a direct link to the United Kingdom via Canada: the undersea cable was laid from Vancouver to Fanning Island in the North Pacific Ocean, then on to Fiji and Norfolk Island, whereupon it forked to go to Queensland and New Zealand, the New Zealand branch came ashore at Cable Bay in Northland, although in 1912 it was redirected to Auckland's Takapuna Beach. While telegraphy was mostly used for business purposes and relaying news, it meant a message could now be transmitted to or from England in under 30 minutes.

The image of clasped hands reuniting those separated by distance was a popular motif on cards around this time (see pages 80 and 104). The quote on this card is an adaptation of a poem by Henry Wadsworth Longfellow, published in 1849 as the dedication to a book of poetry called *The Seaside and the Fireside*. The original poem, about friends separated by distance, reads:

Kind messages, that pass from land to land,
Kind letters, that betray the heart's deep history,
In which we feel the pressure of a hand,
One touch of fire, and all the rest is mystery!

Remembrance flashed from land to land is like the pressure of a hand. [Christmas postcard. ca 1900]
Photolithograph, 89 x 138 mm
Eph-B-POSTCARD-Vol-12-097

CA 1900 • KENNETT WATKINS
A NATIVE PET

Artist Kennett Watkins is probably best known for his somewhat romantic paintings of historical events, but in the early 1900s he turned his hand to a series of greeting cards featuring Maori subjects.

The Christmas card showing *A Native Pet* was one of a series produced by the Wanganui firm of AD Willis (see page 28), which included *A Maori Pa*, *Preparing Dinner* (showing a Maori woman cooking on an open fire outside a whare), *Maori Hospitality* and *A Maori Challenge*. The back of each card includes a short explanation of the custom it depicts: this card describes the use of decoy kaka, tethered to branches, to catch other birds. The unknown writer also notes:

> *This is the regular Maori way of carrying children; and there can be no question that it is far more comfortable, for both mother and child, than the European fashion.*

Born in India to a British army officer, Watkins was educated in England and studied art in Europe before emigrating to New Zealand in 1873. He initially worked as a photographer based in the Bay of Islands, taking tinplate photographs of Maori, and married the granddaughter of pioneer missionary Richard Davis. Watkins, who painted in watercolour and oils, worked as an artist from the late 1870s and exhibited with the Auckland Society of Arts from 1881 to 1915.

He also taught art, as principal of the Auckland Free School of Art, set up by John Logan Campbell in 1878, and at Auckland Grammar and Girls' Grammar schools. His paintings of historical subjects include *The Legend of the Voyage to New Zealand*, showing the arrival of the first Maori canoes; *The Death of Major Von Tempsky at Te-Ngutu-o-te-Manu*; *The Phantom Canoe: a Legend of Lake Tarawera* and *The Burning of the* Boyd, painted with Louis Steele.

Watkins, Kennett 1847–1933
A native pet. [Printed by] A.D. Willis;
[drawn? by] K.W. Wanganui [n.d.]
Chromolithograph, 144 x 105 mm
E-279-q-020

A Peaceful Christmas.

A Native Pet.

1900s
NZ Christmas

This Christmas card from the early 1900s shows one of the most popular and enduring New Zealand symbols, the fern.

By the early 1900s, New Zealand was developing its own identity, separate from but still closely linked to Mother England. New Zealand's official symbol was declared to be the Southern Cross in 1869, but the fern leaf had become an unofficial symbol of national identity as early as the 1880s, when the first New Zealand rugby teams to play overseas adopted it as a symbol on their jerseys. Early teams wore blue uniforms with a gold fern, but by the time the first New Zealand 'Natives' rugby team was assembled in 1888, they bore a silver fern on their shirts and caps. This team, mostly Maori but with five Pakeha members, played 107 rugby matches in New Zealand, Australia and Great Britain in 1888–89, winning 78 — as well as being called on to play eight games of Australian Rules football and two of soccer. The silver fern was adopted again by the 1905 'Originals' on their all-black uniforms, and it remains there to this day.

The name 'Fern Leaf' and a fern symbol were trademarked for use on exported dairy produce as early as 1893, and New Zealand soldiers in the Boer War (see page 50) wore fern-leaf hat badges. A wreath of fern leaves framed the 'Onwards' badges worn by soldiers of the New Zealand Expeditionary Force in the First and Second World Wars, and the leaf symbol marks the graves of New Zealand servicemen overseas. In 1908, when New Zealand was declared a dominion, a fern-leaf wreath replaced the traditional laurel wreath on the governor's official ensign.

Other New Zealand symbols over time have included the moa, and of course the kiwi. The first cartoons depicting the country as a kiwi, rather than earlier motifs such as a small boy or a lion cub, appeared in 1905, although New Zealanders did not begin to be called 'Kiwis' until the First World War.

N. Z. Christmas. [Fern. Card. 1900-1919]
Chromolithograph, on folded card, 87 x 92 mm, with green cord tie down spine and inserted page for greeting
Eph-A-CARDS-Christmas-1900/1919-02

1900s
To greet you for a right happy Christmas

Sending and receiving Christmas cards became a tradition in the 1840s, brought to New Zealand by the first European settlers.

The first commercial Christmas cards were sent in 1843 by Henry Cole, later the founder of London's Victoria and Albert Museum, who found himself with the familiar dilemma of having too many people to send Christmas greetings to and not enough time. He printed 1000 copies of a card designed by his friend John Calcott Horsley, and sold those he didn't use for sixpence each — a luxury purchase at a time when postage was one penny per letter.

The practice caught on, and New Zealand printing firms were quick to start producing their own, often with a local flavour or accentuating the differences between a southern hemisphere summer Christmas and a traditional winter season. Firms such as AD Willis (see page 28) produced ranges featuring New Zealand scenes and events such as the eruption of Mount Tarawera, only a few years after large companies in America had started commercial production of cards. The more well-to-do often had personalised cards printed with their name and address inside.

The Alexander Turnbull Library holds a large collection of Christmas and other greeting cards, including the McCarthy collection of more than 200 cards from the late nineteenth and early twentieth centuries. This fold-out card includes a rather sentimental but typical poem of the time:

> *The sweet and gracious time is here,*
> *To every gentle heart so dear,*
> *Its promises with you remain*
> *Till happy Christmas comes again!*

Best wishes. To greet you for a right happy Christmas. [Card, closed. 1900–1910?] Chromolithograph, on folded card, 142 x 100 mm
Eph-A-CARDS-Christmas-1900/1910-01

Best Wishes

To Dear Jem

To Greet You for a right Happy Christmas

From Louie

Greeting.

The sweet and gracious
time is here,
To every gentle
heart so dear,
Its promises with
you remain
Till happy Christmas
comes again!

H. M. Burnside

1901
DIC Christmas flyer

This Christmas flyer for 1901 from the DIC department store had a Japanese theme, featuring toys, books, fancy goods and 'unique and artistic novelties', ranging in price from sixpence to 20 guineas.

While it assures walk-in and mail-order customers that no one will be pressed to buy, the flyer notes:

The variety and display is quite unsurpassed by any yet made in New Zealand and being specifically selected for presentation purposes from the home markets, America, Japan and the East will be found well worth a visit of inspection.

The first two decades of the twentieth century were the heyday of New Zealand's iconic department stores. These multi-storeyed temples of consumption were the centrepieces of many towns and cities, offering not only a range of goods but also an experience for the shopper.

The DIC — its full name the Drapery Importing Company of New Zealand — was established in Dunedin in 1884 by Bendix Hallenstein, initially as a co-operative store. Hallenstein was a German Jew who emigrated to New Zealand via the Australian goldfields in 1863, and built up a small empire of grocery and drapery stores in Southland and Central Otago. In 1873 he set up New Zealand's first clothing factory and, to retail his products, the Hallensteins chain of menswear stores throughout the country.

The DIC became one of New Zealand's best-known department stores. As well as its flagship store in Dunedin, by 1901 the company also had stores in Christchurch and Wellington. When the new Wellington branch opened in 1929, during the company's heyday, it had New Zealand's first escalator — 25 years before the first escalator was installed in Auckland, at Farmers Trading Company.

The DIC brand disappeared in the 1980s when the company was bought by Arthur Barnett, another iconic Dunedin store, established in 1903, but Hallensteins is still going strong today, as part of the Hallenstein Glasson group.

*D.I.C Xmas 1901. The D.I.C. have much pleasure in inviting you and your friends to inspect their magnificent stock of toys, books, fancy goods, and unique & artistic novelties suitable for Xmas and New Year gifts. The D.I.C. Dunedin, Christchurch, & Wellington. [Pamphlet]. 1901.
Letterpress and Japanese woodblock print, on Japanese paper 203 x 290 mm
Eph-B-RETAIL-1901-01*

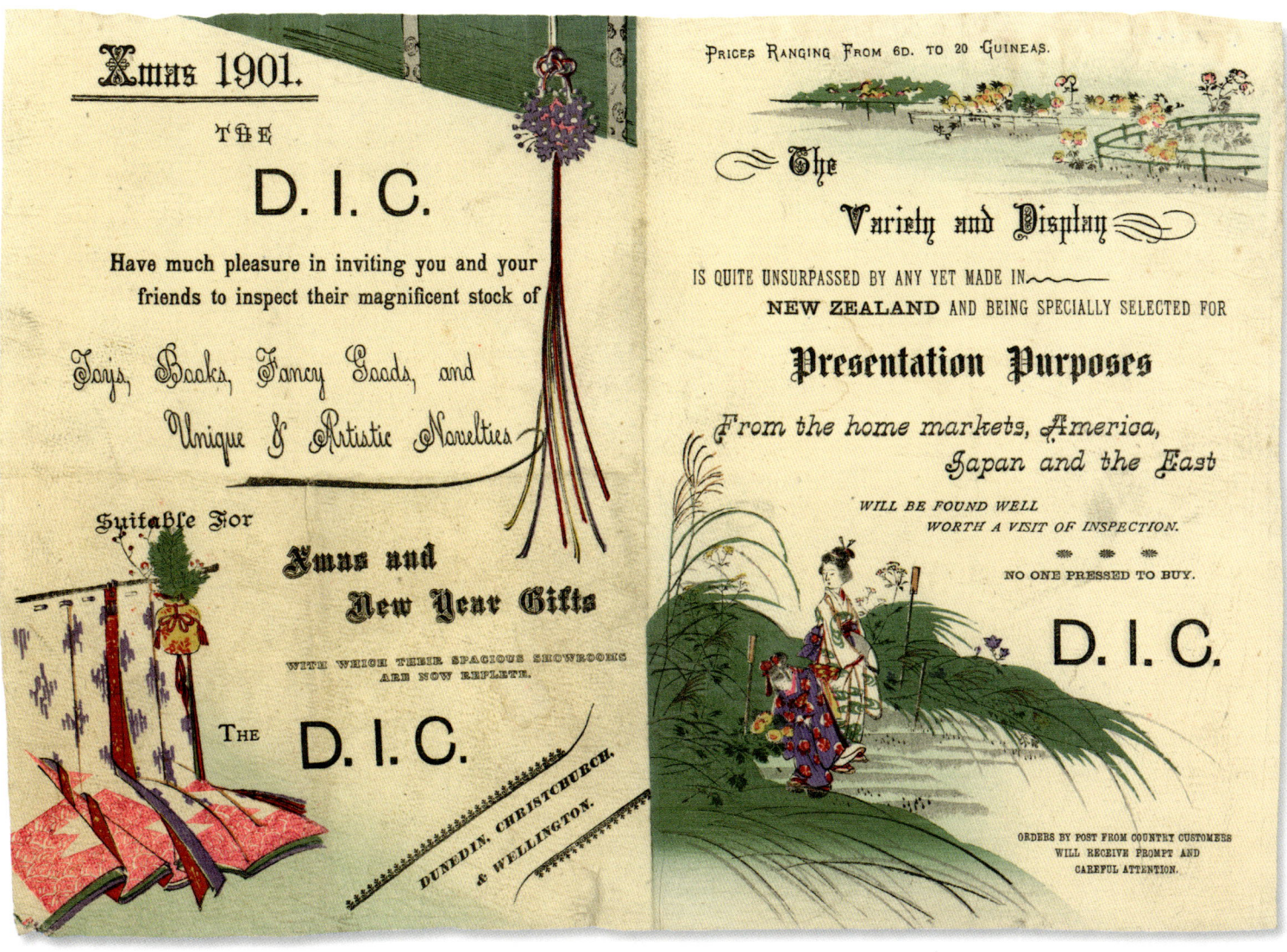

Xmas 1901.

The **D.I.C.**

Have much pleasure in inviting you and your friends to inspect their magnificent stock of

Toys, Books, Fancy Goods, and Unique & Artistic Novelties

Suitable for

Xmas and New Year Gifts

WITH WHICH THEIR SPACIOUS SHOWROOMS ARE NOW REPLETE.

The **D.I.C.**

DUNEDIN, CHRISTCHURCH, & WELLINGTON.

PRICES RANGING FROM 6D. TO 20 GUINEAS.

The **Variety and Display**

IS QUITE UNSURPASSED BY ANY YET MADE IN

NEW ZEALAND AND BEING SPECIALLY SELECTED FOR

Presentation Purposes

From the home markets, America, Japan and the East

WILL BE FOUND WELL WORTH A VISIT OF INSPECTION.

NO ONE PRESSED TO BUY.

D.I.C.

ORDERS BY POST FROM COUNTRY CUSTOMERS WILL RECEIVE PROMPT AND CAREFUL ATTENTION.

1901 • BENONI WHITE
CHRISTMAS GREETINGS FROM THE OFFICERS OF THE GENERAL POST OFFICE

Perhaps because most people had close relatives overseas, New Zealand was a great nation of letter-writers, as this Christmas card from the officers of the General Post Office showed.

The figures inside this romantic-looking card attest to the booming postal business. Universal penny postage had been introduced at the start of 1901 — all letters, national and international, cost just one penny to send — and despite government fears of a loss of revenue, a rise in postal volumes kept the coffers full. By the end of 1900 the Post and Telegraph Department employed 3715 people, up from 3473 the year before. There were 1782 post, telegraph and telephone offices (compared with 986 Post Shops and Post Centres today) and a staggering 36 million letters, 16 million parcels and 1.8 million postcards were posted, by a population of less than a million people. Nearly four million telegrams were forwarded, along 7249 miles (11,666 km) of telegraph line and 20,492 miles (32,979 km) of wire. The department turned a healthy profit, too, with £503,835 worth of income and £418,271 expenditure — a handsome profit of £85,564, the equivalent of about $6.5 million today.

This card, with its image of Christmas greetings speeding over sea and land and down the telegraph wires, was produced by the Wanganui firm of AD Willis (see page 28) and designed by Benoni White, a lithographer, commercial artist and photographer. White was born in Wiltshire in 1858, and at the age of about 30 eloped with the daughter of a landed Irishman. His original surname was Lytton-White, but he does not seem to have used his full name in New Zealand, to where he emigrated without his wife and four children in 1900. He travelled widely around the country, taking photographs for the New Zealand Tourism Department, and during the Second World War was the oldest member of the New Zealand Home Guard.

Chief Post Office (Wellington)
Christmas greetings and hearty good wishes for the New Year, from the officers of the General Post Office, Wellington, N.Z. / [Benoni] White del. et lith. A.D. Willis, Wanganui, N.Z. 1901.
Chromolithograph, on folded card, 187 x 244 mm
Eph-A-CARDS-Christmas-1901-011900/1919-02

1902 · Auckland Weekly News Christmas Number

Weekly News, *Christmas 1902*
N-P 1428 COVER

This romantic view of a Maoriland maiden and flowering manuka graced the cover of the Christmas 1902 edition of the *Auckland Weekly News*, one of the best loved of New Zealand's early publications.

Although now thought of as a scrub plant or a garden shrub, manuka was once considered as appropriate as a 'Christmas flower' as the pohutukawa. It was described as late as the 1930s as 'perhaps the most familiar of all the New Zealand native flowers' (see page 122).

The *Weekly News* was a tabloid published by the same company that established one of Auckland's first newspapers, the *Southern Cross*. This paper was set up by William Brown, the business partner of John Logan Campbell (see page 72). Despite an early disruption in publishing due to the War in the North, the *Southern Cross* became a daily by 1862 and the company started publishing the *Weekly News* in 1863. Like many newspapers of the time, the *Southern Cross* was an unashamedly political vehicle, promoting the interests of land claimants and opposing governor George Grey in the 1860s. The *Weekly News* was a more popular paper, targeting rural readers with a range of articles, features and illustrations that provided a snapshot of the nation.

In 1876 the company was bought by Alfred Horton, who went into partnership with the Wilson brothers, co-owners of *The New Zealand Herald*, which had also been set up in 1863. The *Weekly News* was merged with the *Weekly Herald* to become the *Auckland Weekly News*, and it went from strength to strength into the early decades of the twentieth century. The newspaper was known for its pink cover, and its pages were often reused as wallpaper in remote farmhouses.

From the late 1800s it also produced regular colour supplements, such as reproductions of paintings. This Christmas edition came with a chromolithographed print of a painting by Charles Frederick Goldie entitled *Day dreams; Christmas time in Maoriland*. The *Weekly News* survived bravely into the mid-twentieth century when other similar papers faltered, before closing down in 1971.

PRICE ONE SHILLING

AUCKLAND WEEKLY NEWS
Christmas Number.
1902.

Wilson & Horton Lith. Auckland

1902 • Henry Winkelmann
A merry Christmas 'Kia Ora'

The 'Christmas cruise' was a tradition for many New Zealand yachtsmen and women, making the most of the mostly benign summer weather to voyage forth in craft that would be considered scarcely seaworthy today. These images from a summer cruise by photographer Henry Winkelmann and several of his friends capture the mood of a simpler time.

Winkelmann, born in England but of German descent, came to New Zealand in 1878 at the age of 18. He is considered New Zealand's foremost maritime photographer of the early 1900s, but as well as his iconic pictures of early racing yachts he also photographed landscapes and people.

An early adventure in the Pacific resulted in Winkelmann being marooned for eight months while trying to take possession of a guano island for a shipping company. Following this he worked for the Bank of New Zealand and as a shipping agent before setting up a photography studio in Victoria Arcade in Queen Street, Auckland, in 1901. He had become involved in yachting in the 1890s through the Horton family, co-owners of *The New Zealand Herald* (see page 66), and took a huge portfolio of classic yachting photographs in the 1900s and 1910s.

The images on this card were taken by Winkelmann in 1902 during a cruise aboard a large schooner called *Greyhound*, owned by the Subritzky family, with Herbert Subritzky as master. The crew of five first sailed from Russell across the Bay of Islands to Waitangi, where they visited a meeting house and photographed themselves climbing a memorial plinth. They then sailed north to Whangaroa Harbour, where Winkelmann photographed the rock known as St Paul, behind the township, and Lane and Brown's timber and shipbuilding yard at Totara North. After this the party travelled to Awanui on the Rangaunu Harbour and overland to Ahipara on the west coast.

Collage of nine coastal scenes and activities, created as a 1902 Christmas card.
Photography by Henry Winkelmann (1860–1931)
Henry Winkelmann Collection
PAColl-3097-1

1903
DIX'S GAIETY COMPANY
THE HOUSE THAT JACK BUILT

The tradition of the Christmas pantomime was brought to the new colony by English immigrants. Pantomimes, which became popular during the Victorian era, are usually based on a traditional tale with the addition of contemporary references and humour; they feature such conventions as the main young male character being played by a woman, a pantomime dame, audience participation, slapstick and innuendo.

The 1903 season of *The House that Jack Built*, staged by Percy Dix, was in this traditional style. Miss Emmie Smith played Jack, 'the quickest builder on record', Old Mother Hubbard was played by Tod Callaway in drag, and the cast list featured characters such as Mammon ('the evil spirit of the age'), Truth, Industry, Hope and Puck, 'the merry imp of mischief'. To give the performance a local twist, the ogre ('a terrible customer') sets Jack the challenge of building 'an up-to-date Town Hall for Wellington in one short night' ('and not before it's wanted', adds another character). The building is miraculously constructed by a band of fairy workmen in 'the Great Housebuilding Scene' in Act III, and Jack is set free. The show, staged at Wellington's Theatre Royal, also promised 'gorgeous scenery, surpassing anything hitherto seen'.

Dix's Gaiety Company was one of two competing vaudeville companies in New Zealand at the turn of the twentieth century. Dix, who was born in Launceston, Tasmania (coincidentally also the home town of the Pollards; see page 44), was originally a tea merchant in Auckland but set up a theatre company in 1899. He staged vaudeville-style variety shows in the main centres for several years, and became 'one of the institutions of the colony'. However, fierce competition with the Fuller family forced him to close down his operations in Auckland, Dunedin and Christchurch, followed by Wellington in 1905. He returned to Australia and set up a new vaudeville company in Newcastle, New South Wales.

Theatre Royal (Wellington)
Grand Xmas annual 1903–4 "The house that Jack built"; an up to date version of a good old English Xmas pantomime. Printed by the N.Z. Times Co., Wellington, 1903.
[Programme]
Programme of 36 pages, 185 x 217 mm
Eph-A-PANTOMIME-1903-01

Keep it in the House. Ferguson's Ten-Year-Old P. & O. Whisky. Its purity & Mildness specially adapt it for home use..........

Come at Last..... Ferguson's Superb P. & O. Whisky. 10 years old. Pure and Mellow. Insist on getting it.......

1903
A Merry Christmas & Happy New Year to us all

Having a few drinks has long been a Christmas tradition, and immigrants to New Zealand were quick to establish breweries and distilleries to meet the demand for this and other occasions.

Campbell & Ehrenfried was one of Auckland's pioneer wine and spirit companies and brewers. It was established by settler and businessman John Logan Campbell, known as 'the father of Auckland' for his prominent role in the early days of the city, and brewer Louis Ehrenfried.

Campbell was one of the first Europeans to live in Auckland, setting up camp on the shores of the Waitemata just days after the it was declared the site of the country's new capital in 1840. He established the Domain Brewery in the 1880s, and was soon producing 210 hogsheads of beer a week. Campbell later became one of Auckland's best-known civic and business leaders and philanthropists.

Louis Ehrenfried was a German Jew who had emigrated to New Zealand via the Australian goldfields with his brother Bernard and sister Catherine. Louis and Bernard moved to the Thames goldfields and set themselves up as brewers. Bernard died in 1869 and Louis later took on his nephew, Catherine's son Arthur Myers, moving his brewing operation to Auckland in 1885. Ten years later the firm merged with Campbell's liquor business, forming Campbell & Ehrenfried, a brewing and merchant company with 100 employees. Ehrenfried died just as the merger was completed, leaving Myers, the grandfather of one of New Zealand's most successful businessmen, Sir Douglas Myers, the managing director of the new firm at the age of only 30.

Operations were initially concentrated on the Albert Brewery in Queen Street, then in 1915 the company merged with the Lion Brewery, another pioneer operation run by the Seccombe family. In 1923 Lion merged with nine other breweries around the country to form New Zealand Breweries, under the chairmanship of Alfred Bankart, formerly the secretary and later managing director of Campbell & Ehrenfried.

Campbell & Ehrenfried Company Ltd
Campbell & Ehrenfried Co. Ltd, Wine & spirit merchants, brewers & bottlers. A merry Christmas & a happy New Year to us all. Puriri natural mineral water. [1903] from New Zealand Graphic, Xmas 1903, *inside back cover*
Lithograph on page 380 x 260 mm (approx)
PUBL-0126-1903-12-001

Kia Ora. To [TH Hamer Esq], with the compliments of the Prime Minister. Wishing you a Merry Christmas & a Happy New Year. Wellington, New Zealand. Xmas, 1905. New Year, 1906. [Signed] RJ Seddon. [Christmas booklet cover]. 1905. Photolithograph on cover of booklet of 8 pages, 145 x 226 mm Eph-A-CARDS-Christmas-Seddon-1905-cover.

1905
KIA ORA, WITH THE COMPLIMENTS OF THE PRIME MINISTER

Richard Seddon's Liberal government brought in an era of massive social change for New Zealand at the end of the nineteenth century and the beginning of the twentieth. Each year he was in office, Seddon's official Christmas card showcased the government's achievements and commemorated current events.

The Liberals, originally led by John Ballance, swept to power in 1890 and ruled until 1912. Seddon, widely known as 'King Dick', became leader after Ballance's death in 1893, and remained in charge until his own death in 1906. The Liberals are often credited with establishing New Zealand's famous welfare state; with Seddon as premier and prime minister, legislation was passed on a wide range of social issues: old-age pensions, land ownership, the care of mothers and babies, industrial relations and workplace regulation.

The Alexander Turnbull Library holds Seddon's illustrated cards for 1897, 1899 (see page 50) and 1900–1905. The Christmas card booklet for 1905–New Year 1906 starts with a sketch contrasting Christmas 'in Ye Olde Land' and in New Zealand, followed by photographs of the 1905 rugby team touring Britain — the team that became known as 'The Originals' and gave rise to the name All Blacks. It also features photographs of Victoria College, Wellington (now Victoria University); 'a New Zealand state workman's home'; nurses and babies at a maternity home; and Seddon turning the first sod at the Port Chalmers Dock, Dunedin, and laying the foundation stone for the New Zealand International Exhibition.

The International Exhibition in Christchurch was Seddon's brainchild, designed to showcase this country as 'the social laboratory of the world'. Unfortunately he did not live to see it; he died in June 1906, while returning by ship to what he called 'God's own country' after a round of negotiations and meetings in Sydney.

CA 1905 • AP GODBER
COMPLIMENTS OF THE SEASON

Images of the Rimutaka railway incline might seem to be an unusual subject for a Christmas card, but it was a location dear to the heart of this card's creator, Albert Percy Godber.

Godber was an amateur photographer and artist, volunteer firefighter, beekeeper and inveterate trainspotter who worked at the Petone railway workshops. Godber visited the Alexander Turnbull Library regularly, on Fridays, and after his death in 1949 he left his collection of around 2000 photographs and drawings, as well as correspondence, diaries and reminiscences, many of a railway nature, to the library. His photographs include many images of the Petone area, where the Godber family lived in the early decades of last century. Godber was also interested in Maori customs and history, and the library holds his notes on the meanings of Maori placenames as well as sketches of rafter patterns from churches such as the historic Rangiatea at Otaki, which was destroyed by fire in 1995.

The card features a montage of images of the Rimutaka Incline, one of New Zealand's most striking feats of railway engineering. A railway connection between Upper Hutt and Featherston in the Wairarapa was first built in 1878. While the Rimutaka Range could be summited using regular railway construction methods on the Upper Hutt side, the 1:15 gradient descending to the Wairarapa Valley was so steep a Fell centre-rail system had to be installed to enable specially fitted locomotives to negotiate the steep grade.

The Fell system was used on the Rimutakas far longer than anywhere else in the world. The railway operated until 1955, when a tunnel through the Rimutaka Range was opened, and the rails of the incline taken up. Parts of the route are now open to walkers and mountain-bikers, and the railway is under restoration by a trust, which hopes to reopen it as a tourist attraction.

Christmas card designed by AP Godber, using a montage of images of railway interest relating to the Rimutaka Incline. Circa 1905? Photographs by Albert Percy Godber (1875–1949)
Dry plate glass negative 6.5 x 4.75 inches
AP Godber Collection
APG-1606-1/2-G

New Zealand Free Lance, Volume VIII, Issue 391, 28 December 1907, page 17
N-P1429-17

1907 • WILLIAM BLOMFIELD
CHRISTMAS IN FERNLAND AND AT HOME

The reversal of the seasons between many New Zealand settlers' British 'homeland' and their new home Down Under was perhaps thrown into most stark relief at Christmas.

This full-page cartoon from *The New Zealand Free Lance* plays on this contrast, highlighting the delights of a summer Christmas in 'Fernland'. At the masthead, holidaying New Zealanders are shown enjoying the great outdoors, camping and fishing, while at the foot of the page is the contrast of Christmas 'at Home', a snowy vista complete with ice skaters.

The cartoons are by William Blomfield (see page 40), and contrast cricket, tennis and sailing with ice skating and rugby, while the somewhat sentimental poem describes the differences between Christmas in the two lands:

See o'er the bay the snow-white sails are shining,
Where skim the yachts like birds beneath the blue,
See in yon bush, where red, red rata twining
Its glorious wealth of flowers enchants the view . . .
Here 'neath our Southern summer's vault of azure
We think of them wrapped in the winter's snow,
And wish for them that days of health and pleasure
May keep their hearts like ours in kindling glow.

One of the country's most popular pictorials, *The New Zealand Free Lance* was first published in Wellington in 1900 and came out weekly until 1960, when it was incorporated into the *Auckland Weekly News* (see page 66). It featured stories on local social and sporting events as well as politics and New Zealand's natural wonders. This edition, Volume VIII, Issue 391, included stories on the railway workshops voting to stay outside the provisions of the Industrial Conciliation and Arbitration Act, 'Our Charitable Aid Boards: are they creating pauperism?', raceday tips and a review of the Wellington Musical Union's production of *Israel in Egypt*.

Christmas in Fernland

Christmas is here, the time of happy meeting,
And sweet forgetfulness of days of care,
When from afar our dear ones come with greeting—
The happiest, gladdest season of the year.

A time of memories and sweet reflection,
Recalling songs and faces from the past,
The loves, and golden days of retrospection
Surge like some tide from out the shadows vast.

Here 'neath some shady tree in restful leisure
Amid the glory of our Southern lands,
We spend in peace the hours of Christmas pleasure
While speed away the years' quick-running sands.

The youth and maiden in the forest bowers
Gather fair Nature's offerings, or enjoy
The festive picnic, deck'd with summer flowers
Whilst merry sport the fleeting hours employ.

See o'er the bay the snow-white sails are shining,
Where skim the yachts like birds beneath the blue,
See in yon bush, where red, red rata twining
Its glorious wealth of flowers enchants the view.

The lusty youth, in manly sports engaging,
Heightens the pleasant scene with comely grace,
'Tis summer, and the sunlight all assuaging
Lends Christmas joy that care cannot efface.

But memory points us back to years now vanished,
Where danced the Yule-fire in the after-glow,
When, with the wintry day all care was banished,
And merry tales laughed out the driving snow.

There on the frozen moorland or the river
The vigorous pastimes warmed the sluggish blood,
The Christmas joys with friends of yore who never
Shall hail again the time in joyous mood.

When o'er the earth the still white mantle glistened,
And merrily the Christmas bells were rung,
Whilst for the call of friends beloved we listened,
Or cheered them when the Noel song was sung.

Here 'neath our Southern summer's vault of azure
We think of them wrapped in the winter's snow,
And wish for them that days of health and pleasure
May keep their hearts like ours in kindling glow.

Keep them, whilst passing years on isle or ocean,
Hold us—one people, link'd in bonds of peace—
Faithful of heart, in true and strong devotion
Till the long rest, when all our journeys cease.

CA 1910
OUR HEARTS IN MAORILAND TO-DAY . . .

The close relationship between New Zealand and Great Britain was a common theme in Christmas cards at the turn of the century. This card again draws on the image of clasped hands (see pages 54 and 104) to represent a connection between family and friends parted by great distance.

The card bears the poem:
> *Our hearts in Maoriland to-day*
> *Remember loved ones far away.*
> *And so with hands across the sea*
> *Kia-ora is my wish for thee.*

Featuring images of Maori maidens — and the main trunk railway line — to represent New Zealand, and St Paul's Cathedral in London to represent the Motherland, the hand-tinted card was produced in England. It was sent from New Zealand to J and R Robinson of Little Norton, Bradford, Yorkshire. On the back, in the 'space for communication in New Zealand or the British Empire', is written: 'Wishing you a downright happy Christmas and a most prosperous New Year from Lilian Briggs and Ida Lilian Robinson, love to all'.

This card was featured in a National Library exhibition in 1988 of materials related to New Zealand's best-known short-story writer, Katherine Mansfield. *Hearts & Minds* showcased the library's wealth of Mansfield-related letters and other written material, as well as material not directly connected to Mansfield that illuminated the social and cultural milieu in which she moved. Mansfield moved to London in 1908 and never returned to New Zealand.

37

Kia Ora. Our hearts in Maoriland today . . .
F.T. series No. G 166. Protected. New Zealand postcard (carte postale). Made in England [ca 1910].
Photograph, on postcard 86 x 136 mm
Eph-POSTCARD-Hearts-and-Minds-04

1910s
Christmas and New Year novelty cheques

Despite the fact that in New Zealand the seasons were the opposite of those in Europe, with the turning of the year in midsummer rather than the dead of winter, wishes for Christmas and the new year remained universal.

These samples of two attractive novelty gift cheques produced by Christchurch printer James Rodger & Co wish the recipients health, happiness, prosperity and success during a difficult decade that would be marred by war and disease.

The cheque issued by The Bank of Prosperity (top) wishes the recipient 'good fortune and good cheer throughout the coming year', with a value of 'three hundred and sixty-five days of Unbroken Prosperity together with health and happiness'. It is decorated with a recognisably New Zealand scene of a lake framed by cabbage trees and flax, but the border is made up of more traditional Christmas flora: holly leaves and berries. In the centre a female figure holds an overflowing cornucopia, symbolising abundance.

The Consolidated Bank of Success cheque pays to the bearer 'three hundred and sixty-five days of Prosperity, Good Luck and Happiness'. The banner at the top, supported by the figures of Zealandia — a graphic representation of the young nation as a kind of daughter of Britannia — and a Maori chief, bears the greeting:

May courage and good health your course keep clear,

And fortune favour you through all the year

In the centre of the banner is a representation of New Zealand's new coat of arms, granted by royal warrant in 1911. The upper left quadrant shows the Southern Cross, with a wheat sheaf below representing the agricultural industry. On the right, a slung-up sheep represents farming, with crossed hammers below it representing mining. In the centre are three ships, symbolising the importance of sea trade to New Zealand.

The Alexander Turnbull Library also holds a third cheque of this type, issued in 1917, showing a soldier flanked by a New Zealand view and a battle scene. This time the cheque's value is simply 'a year of heart's desire and happiness'.

James Rodger & Co (Firm)
Two draft novelty Christmas and New Year gift cheques / printed by James Rodger & Co. Christchurch. 191[0s].
Coloured lithographs, with perforated left edge, each 120 x 233 mm
Eph-A-CARDS-New-Year-1910s-01

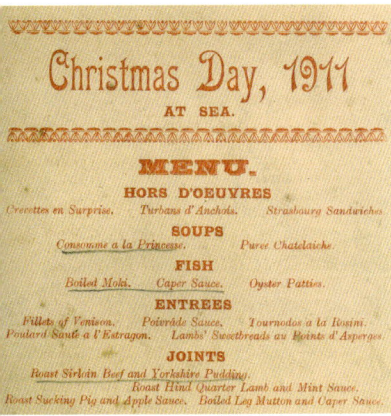

T.S.S. 'Ulimaroa'
Christmas Day, 1911 at sea. Menu. 1911.
Letterpress, on card 255 x 138 mm
Eph-B-SHIP-1911-01

1911
Christmas Day menu, TSS *Ulimaroa*

Christmas at sea was a special occasion for the trans-Tasman passengers aboard TSS *Ulimaroa*, with a grand 11-course dinner being offered.

The elaborate menu included familiar Christmas fare such as roast turkey, roast goose and plum pudding, and more unusual offerings such as 'tournados à la Rosini', curried prawns and rice with Bombay duck, and Nesselrode pudding, an ice pudding made with roasted chestnuts poached in syrup.

The 5828-ton turbine steamship (TSS) *Ulimaroa* was built in 1908. She was one of the best-known steamers of the Huddart Parker fleet, which operated around the Australian coast and on the trans-Tasman route. The name *Ulimaroa* had been recorded by early explorers as a name for Australia; possibly of Polynesian or Maori origin, it became in turn the name of a house lived in by shipowner John Traill, one of the founders of Huddart Parker. When launched, *Ulimaroa* was the company's largest liner, departing on her maiden voyage from Sydney to New Zealand ports in February 1908. She offered cabin accommodation for 292 first-class and 121 second-class passengers.

Two shipboard newspapers published on this voyage, held by the Alexander Turnbull Library, feature a front-page announcement that the ship carried equipment to enable wireless communication with Sydney and Wellington while at sea. At this time six Huddart Parker steamers were fitted with wireless telegraph: *Zealandia*, *Ulimaroa*, *Riverina*, *Wimmera*, *Victoria* and *Westralia*.

Following the outbreak of the First World War, six Huddart Parker ships were requisitioned for war service, with *Ulimaroa* and *Zealandia* used as troopships carrying soldiers to the battlefields of Europe. In 1918, *Wimmera* sank after hitting a mine between Auckland and Sydney, with the loss of 26 crew. *Ulimaroa* was painted in camouflage colours and made five trips from New Zealand to Egypt, returning with wounded soldiers. She returned to service on Australian routes after the war until being scrapped in 1934.

T.S.S. "ULIMAROA."

Christmas Day, 1911
AT SEA.

MENU.

HORS D'OEUVRES
Crevettes en Surprise. Turbans d'Anchois. Strasbourg Sandwiches.

SOUPS
Consomme a la Princesse. Puree Chatelaiche.

FISH
Boiled Moki. Caper Sauce. Oyster Patties.

ENTREES
Fillets of Venison. Poivrâde Sauce. Tournodos a la Rosini.
Poulard Sauté a l'Estragon. Lambs' Sweetbreads au Points d'Asperges.

JOINTS
Roast Sirloin Beef and Yorkshire Pudding.
Roast Hind Quarter Lamb and Mint Sauce.
Roast Sucking Pig and Apple Sauce. Boiled Leg Mutton and Caper Sauce.

POULTRY
Roast Turkey a la Chipolata. Roast Goose and Savoury Sauce.

GAME
Roast Pheasant and Bread Sauce.

CURRY
Prawns and Rice with Bombay Duck.

VEGETABLES
French Beans. Mashed White Turnips. Baked and Boiled Potatoes.

SWEETS
Plum Pudding. Hard and Cognac Sauce. Fruit Tart. Caramel Cream.
Nesselrode Pudding. Gateaux au Cognac. Nougât a la Chantilly.
Chartreuse d'Ananas.

SAVOURY
Pompadours a la Portugaise.

Fruit en Season. Café.

1912 • Arthur Northwood
Christmas in the Far North of New Zealand

It is the quintessential New Zealand Christmas scene: pohutukawa blazing, children in a boat, the calm waters of a beautiful Northland harbour. Such a scene would have been familiar to photographer Arthur Northwood, who was brought up at Houhora, in the Far North.

The hand-coloured image appeared as a supplement to the Christmas edition of the *Auckland Weekly News* in 1912 (see page 66). Alexander Turnbull Library holds a significant collection of original images taken by Kaitaia-based photographer Arthur James Northwood and his brothers Richard Alfred and Hubert Charles Northwood. Many show Northland's industries of the early 1900s, such as kauri-gum digging, or kauri logging and farming, as well as local Maori, towns of the north, and current events such as shipwrecks. The bulk of the images held by the Turnbull were taken between 1910 and the 1930s by Arthur Northwood.

The Northwood brothers' father, Richard Arthur Northwood, was an Australian-born pharmacist who came to New Zealand in the 1860s to serve with the Armed Constabulary in the Taranaki phase of the New Zealand Wars. The three Northwood brothers were born at Pukearuhe in Taranaki before the family moved to the Houhora Harbour in the Far North. Richard Northwood senior, a photographer himself, encouraged his sons' interest in the field, arranging for them to study it by correspondence, as well as the practical skill of accountancy.

In 1910 Arthur, the eldest brother, established a studio in Kaitaia. From 1910 Richard Northward junior, an accountant, and Hubert Norwood also operated a photographic studio, called Northwood Brothers, at Kohukohu on the Hokianga Harbour. Hubert also later ran studios in Gisborne and Auckland.

Northwood, Arthur James, 1880–1949
Christmas in the Far North of New Zealand. A. Northwood, photo. Supplement to the Auckland Weekly News, *special Christmas number, 1912.*
Photolithograph, 332 x 464 mm
B-033-005

CHRISTMAS IN THE FAR NORTH OF NEW ZEALAND.

1913 • EDNA CROMPTON
LETTER TO FATHER CHRISTMAS

Letters written to Father Christmas by children today are likely to contain requests for such items as PlayStations, iPods and mobile phones. It was a different story in 1913 when eight-year-old Edna Crompton wrote this missive to the North Pole.

Edna's list was comprehensive. She wanted a doll's head and a small doll's house, 'a box of *good* paints', a picture book, a notebook, a money box and a toy, as well as some Christmas treats — oranges, apples, nuts and a box of chocolates. Those items that Father Christmas 'must be sure to bring' are marked with a tick — everything except the notebook.

Top of Edna's list was a thumb Bible, a miniature, abridged version of the Bible popular with children and collectors. Advances in typesetting, lithography and photographic reproduction made making tiny books like this possible during the Victorian age, and they reached the height of their popularity around the turn of the century.

Perhaps the most poignant aspect of the letter is the postscript: 'don't bring Germans things'. With the outbreak of the First World War just eight months away, the war clouds gathering over Europe had obviously had an impact on the young girl, at the time living in St Helens, Lancashire, in the north of England.

When her father, William Crompton, was called up to serve after the outbreak of war in 1914, Edna, her mother Evelyn, brother Alfred and sister Rhoda were forced to leave their home and live with distant relatives. Although William survived the war, one of Edna's uncles was killed in the Somme in 1916.

Edna emigrated to New Zealand in 1977 and lived in Lowry Bay, Wellington, until her death at the age of 92. Edna's daughter, Wellington journalist Judy Bradwell, found the letter when sorting through papers after her mother's death.

Bradwell, Judy, fl 2003
Family papers
1913, [1950], 1999
fMS-Papers-7627
© Judy Bradwell

Dear Father Christmas,
Please Will you bring me the list which I wright down, and the ones that I tick you must be sure to bring.

1. A thumb Bible ✓
2. A doll's head ✓
   ~~A set of dolls clothes~~
3. A box of good paints ✓
4. A nice picture book ✓
5. A small doll's house ✓
6. Some orang. apples and nuts ✓
7. A box of choclates ✓
8. A good note book ✗
9. A pretty money box ✓
10. A toy ✓

Now I must close a loving from
dont bring Germans things Edna

1915 · Oliver & Varley
Tables set for Christmas dinner, Maymorn camp

Tables set for Christmas dinner, Maymorn camp, Wairarapa
Photograph taken by Oliver and Varley
25 December 1915
ST Allen Collection
1/2-112210-F

By Christmas 1915, New Zealand troops overseas had experienced their first long year of war. These troops celebrating Christmas while in training at Maymorn military camp in Upper Hutt would be among the next echelon dispatched to France as the war dragged on into 1916.

When Great Britain first declared war against Germany in August 1914, New Zealand did not have its own army. However, the government was quick to mobilise its Territorial force and utilise the corps of young men, aged between 14 and 20, who had undergone compulsory military training since its introduction in 1911. Training camps were urgently set up in Featherston in the Wairarapa, at Narrow Neck in Auckland and Awapuni near Palmerston North, with the main camp at Trentham in Upper Hutt.

In October 1914, in the same week the first 8500 members of the First New Zealand Expeditionary Force were dispatched to the Middle East, civilians and volunteers laboured to set up a tent camp at Trentham to house and train 3000 recruits who would be the Second Reinforcements. By March 1915 work had started on building huts on the site, and by July that year there were around 50, housing 8000 men, as well as a comprehensive roading, drainage and sewerage system.

This camp at Maymorn, 7 km up the Hutt Valley from Trentham, was built as an overflow camp on land previously occupied by the Maymorn Timber Company. The sole wooden buildings were the cookhouses, the Army Service Corps stores, the canteens and shops; the men lived under canvas. However, according to Will Lawson's fascinating account of training-camp life, *Historic Trentham*, published in 1918, 'In every way May Morn was a model camp, especially as regards the sanitary arrangements'. It was the home of the 3rd and 4th Battalions of the New Zealand Rifle Brigade, then the 11th Infantry Reinforcements, until the camp was closed in January 1916.

1915 • LAURIE C MACKIE
CHRISTMAS IN A DUG-OUT, GALLIPOLI

Today, the name Gallipoli is rooted in the national consciousness. At Christmas 1915, it was only just gaining recognition as a word representing horrific loss and wasted lives.

These men in a Gallipoli dug-out in December 1915 would have been photographed not long before the Allied withdrawal from the ill-fated peninsula, on December 20. This was the end of eight months of hell for the New Zealand, Australian and other Allied troops who landed at what became known as Anzac Cove on April 25, 1915.

The Australians landed first, at night, coming ashore to a landscape of steep, unclimbable cliffs and little cover. The New Zealanders followed in the morning, to find scores of dead and wounded Australians lying on the beach. The order was given to 'dig, dig, dig!' so the Anzac soldiers began to create a network of dug-outs to provide a little defence from the Turkish barrage from above. In these rabbit warrens, described by one soldier as looking 'like an ant-heap, swarming with men', they settled down to live in filthy conditions, with inadequate food and water supplies, and experiencing outbreaks of dysentery and other diseases.

Despite several assaults on the Turkish position, including the taking of Chunuk Bair by Colonel William Malone and the Wellington Battalion — a position they were forced to abandon after 36 hours due to lack of back-up from British forces — the Gallipoli operation was declared a failure. After huge troop losses and with winter setting in, the British Army ordered an evacuation by night. Fires were left burning and automatic rifles set up to fire so the retreat would be unnoticed by the Turkish forces occupying the high ground. Of the 8500 New Zealanders who had landed at Gallipoli, more than 2700 had been killed and around 4750 wounded — an 88 per cent casualty rate.

This photograph was probably taken by Laurie C Mackie, a New Zealand soldier who fought at Gallipoli and afterwards in Europe. The Alexander Turnbull Library holds four albums of his images from the battlefields, in many of which he appears.

Christmas celebrations in dug-out, Gallipoli
December 1915
Toned gelatin silver print 5.1 x 7.6 cm
(visible image) mounted on album page
Laurie C Mackie albums
PA1-o-308-22-3

1916
COMPLIMENTS OF THE SEASON FROM FRANCE

If the slaughter at Gallipoli hadn't been enough of a shocking wake-up call, the theatre of war in northern France, where the New Zealand troops were moved to, was even worse. By Christmas 1916, thousands more New Zealanders had been killed and wounded in battle.

Once New Zealand's troops had been withdrawn from Turkey, they were redeployed to the battlefields of the Western Front. Germany had invaded France and Belgium and fighting was fierce in northern France, near Verdun, in early 1916. The British military devised a plan to attack the Germans in the Somme region, 200 km northwest of Verdun, to relieve pressure on the beleaguered French. The Battle of the Somme began with a first offensive in June 1916, followed by a second push in mid-September, which involved New Zealand troops and the use of tanks.

Around 15,000 members of the New Zealand Division, part of XV Corps of the British Fourth Army, were sent into battle at the Somme; after a month in action, nearly 6000 had been wounded and 2000 killed in a mire of mud, corpses and artillery shells. By November 18, 1916, when the British decided to abandon the offensive, around 1.2 million men on both sides had been killed or wounded, yet the Allies had only advanced around 12 km into German-held territory.

Over half the New Zealand Somme dead have no known graves, but they are commemorated on a memorial at the Caterpillar Valley Cemetery near Longueval. The remains of one soldier were returned home in November 2004 and interred in the Tomb of the Unknown Warrior outside New Zealand's National War Memorial.

The Latin motto underneath the gun emblem at the top of the card, the symbol of the Royal New Zealand Artillery, means 'where right and glory lead'. The message on the back of this card is simple: 'To Chris, from Dick, 6/12/16'.

Sparr, fl 1916
Compliments of the season from France, 1916–17. Onward. N.Z. Quo fas et gloria ducunt. [Postcard. 1916]
Offset lithograph, green on white card, 140 x 89 mm
Eph-A-WAR-WI-1916-08

1916
Christmas menu, Sling Camp

After a year of horrendous fighting and loss on the battlefields of Belgium and France, the nation-building battle at Gallipoli was still at the forefront of New Zealand soldiers' minds at Christmas 1916.

This Christmas menu is from the Sergeants' Mess at the New Zealand Army Service Corps Number 6 camp at Sling, near Bulford on the Salisbury Plain in England. It was dedicated to the memory of Gallipoli and the newly minted 'Anzac Day', commemorating the landing in Turkey. The menu for breakfast, dinner, tea and supper shows the men ate well — from liver, bacon and chips for breakfast through a full roast dinner of turkey, beef and chicken to leftover roast, mince pies, jam tarts and beer for supper.

Sling Camp was originally a British military training camp, built as an annexe to the nearby Bulford camp, which was used by New Zealand and Canadian troops from 1914. It was officially known as the 4th New Zealand Infantry Brigade Reserve Camp, although it was nicknamed Anzac Camp, and was used for training new reinforcements and for casualties to regain fitness to return to the front line.

Due to a lack of available troopships at the end of the First World War, there was a delay in some soldiers at Sling Camp being shipped home. After some unrest, the men of the Canterbury Battalion Engineers were put to work carving a giant kiwi in the chalk of the hill above the camp. It was designed by Sergeant-Major Percy Blenkarne of the army's Education Staff, based on a sketch of a specimen kiwi in the British Museum.

The Bulford kiwi is still visible today, at around 127 m high, with a bill 45 m long and the letters 'NZ' below it, 20 m high. For many years it was maintained by the (Australian) Kiwi Shoe Polish company, and it was camouflaged during the Second World War so it could not be used as a landmark for bombing raids.

[Sling Camp (England)] Remember ANZAC, Gallipoli, 25th April, 1915. Christmas 1916, New Year 1917 / [Sergeants' Mess, New Zealand Army Service Corps and Details, No 6 Camp, Sling, Bulford, Salisbury Plain, England. [Menu / list of members]. Bennett Bros, Military Printers, Salisbury [1916]. Folded booklet, 223 x 144 mm with red cord tie.
Eph-A-WAR-WI-1916-02

[Greeting card]. A right loyal greeting. 'Land of our birth, we pledge to thee, Head heart & hand, in the years to be'. Xmas 1916 . . . from Mr & Mrs A. St. N. Hardie. Wanganui, N.Z.
Offset print on folded card with inset page, 90 x 118 mm
Eph-A-CARDS-Christmas-1916-01

1916
A right loyal greeting

The outbreak of the First World War and New Zealand's rush to support Mother England in her fight against the German aggressors brought on a surge of imperial as well as national pride, as reflected in this Christmas card from 1916.

This small card, just 118 mm across, was printed for Mr and Mrs Hardie of Wanganui. It bears the poem:

Land of our birth we pledge to thee
Head heart and hand in the years to be
Be Justice and Peace the whole world o'er
And banished forever the thought of war

Discussions about New Zealand's identity and role in the wider world — either as an outpost of Empire or an independent nation — were common in the late nineteenth and early twentieth centuries, and war in Europe brought the matter strongly to the fore. Bill Massey, New Zealand prime minister from 1912–25, was a staunch imperialist, who believed it was the mission of the Anglo-Saxon people to provide peace and stability in the world as the descendants of one of the lost tribes of Israel. He was quick to volunteer New Zealand troops in Britain's defence at the outbreak of the First World War. Massey formed a wartime coalition government with Liberal Joseph Ward, another imperialist who had pushed for the formation of an imperial defence council in the 1910s. This passion for imperialism was not seen as restricting New Zealand's powers by linking it to Britain but as a way of expanding them, giving the country a say in British foreign and defence policy.

Massey and Ward travelled to Europe in 1916 and visited the New Zealand troops in France, where they were greeted with some cynicism. However, at the 1917 Imperial War Conference they managed to gain an agreement that New Zealand was equal in status and law to Great Britain and was to be consulted about imperial foreign policy.

Scenes at the main hospital camp of the 7th Medical Unit of the Scottish Women's Hospitals for Foreign Service, at Ostrovo, Macedonia, Serbia, during World War I 1916
Agnes Bennett Collection
PAColl-6972-12-20

1916
Dinner, Christmas Day, Ostrovo

Even in the midst of war, the celebration of Christmas has a way of adding a touch of light to dark days. The diary of New Zealand doctor Agnes Bennett records a day of companionship and fun at the Scottish Women's Hospital in Ostrovo, Serbia.

'Our Christmas festivities . . . started before dawn with carol singing,' she wrote. 'The day fortunately turned out fine and at 10 we had a good turn out to service in our very gaily decorated tent with a tree made round the centre pole and lots of coloured paper etc. sent up by the British Red Cross.'

At midday a roast turkey dinner was served to the staff and doctors from neighbouring camps, followed by a long round of toasts. In the late afternoon a meal was served to the Serb orderlies — 'poor old things, so many half decrepit, they did enjoy it. We had a proper Father Christmas and I made an interpreter explain that he came every Christmas to England and because the "Englisky" were here he had come to see them and they all got socks, cigarettes and a card.' Dancing followed, with the Serbs teaching the medical staff a local dance, and at 7 pm the medical staff put on a variety concert. However, the war continued: Bennett adds 'The Bosches [Germans] were above us in the afternoon . . . we hear a good deal of distant bombarding.'

Bennett was born in Australia and trained as a doctor in Scotland before working in Sydney and Wellington. She volunteered for work in the Middle East and then Europe with the outbreak of the First World War, and was appointed commanding officer of the 7th Medical Unit, Scottish Women's Hospitals for Foreign Service, running this field hospital in Macedonia (at the time part of Serbia). Bennett returned to New Zealand after the war and made a significant contribution to maternal and neonatal health here, as well as serving overseas in the Second World War.

S.W.H Ostrovo.

Dinner. Xmas Day 1916.

Ostrovo.

Doctors' Tents. (Harley St.)

1917 • Henry Armytage Sanders
The New Zealand Commander carves the turkey on Christmas Day

By Christmas 1917, New Zealand troops were still at war in Europe. However, some gains had been made and the New Zealand headquarters was now at Chateau Segard, near Ypres, Belgium.

This picture shows the New Zealand divisional commander, Major-General Andrew Hamilton Russell, carving a turkey for officers including British officer Henry Maitland 'Jumbo' Wilson. The photograph was taken by Henry Armytage Sanders, the official NZEF photographer and cinematographer in France and Belgium.

The year 1917 had seen some of the worst fighting and the greatest losses of the First World War. The New Zealand Division had become involved in fighting in Belgium in June 1917, with the Battle of Messines. This offensive was a success, with New Zealand, Australian and British soldiers taking the strategically important ridge and village. The troops then mounted an attack on the ridges at Passchendaele. After several unsuccessful attempts, several major pushes were made in October, including 'the blackest day', October 12, when poor planning and the seemingly endless mud and rain meant the advancing New Zealanders were slaughtered by the Germans: more than 2700 of them, including more than 800 left either dead or dying in no-man's land. The New Zealanders were relieved six days later by Canadian forces, who went on to take Passchendaele, but by mid-November the offensive was abandoned, having gained only about 8 km of enemy territory.

A New Zealand soldier, Private Henry Bourke, wrote home to his mother from Belgium on Christmas Day, 1917:

> . . . this doesn't seem much like Christmas, it is snowing away outside and the ice on the pools is about 8 inches thick . . . A bit of [a mortar] about half an inch square hit me on the shoulder. It went through my overcoat, coat jersey and shirt but stopped at the flannel singlet. It was a good thick singlet and I haven't had a chance of changing it for about a month so I suppose its resisting qualities were improved.

New Zealand Commander carves the turkey on Christmas Day, Chateau Segard, 1917. Photographer: Henry Armytage Sanders
25 Dec 1917
Royal New Zealand Returned and Services' Association Collection
Dry plate glass negative 4.75 x 6.5 inches
1/2-013034-G

1917
HANDS ACROSS THE SEA

As the war in Europe dragged on, many families in New Zealand at Christmas 1917 had to endure yet another festive season with loved ones still far away.

Again, this card uses the imagery of hands clasped across the distance (see pages 54 and 80), bridging the sea between New Zealand and 'somewhere in France' and 'Blighty'. It contrasts the desolation of the battlefields of France with an iconic image of a small, red-roofed New Zealand farmhouse with a view of the sea, surrounded by native flax and cabbage trees.

The front of the card bears the poem:
For England, Home and Beauty,
For Christmas and for you,
With heart and hands across the sea,
Here comes my Greeting true.

The message on the back is brief but poignant, perhaps written between brothers:
Foxton, Sept 24, 1917

Dear Harry
Just a few lines to let you know we are home on our holidays again and I only wish you were hear [sic] too the old farm is looking as well as ever only it is a bit too much for dad to keep it going they are hoping you will soon be home again to look after it well. I hope you are well as it leaves us at present.

I remain
Yours ever
Tom

Postcard. Christmas greetings. Hands across the sea. NZ Postcard published by Frank Duncan & Co., High St., Auckland. [1917] Chromolithograph on card, 91 x 140 mm
Eph-A-CARDS-Christmas-WWI-1917-02

1918
Cheerio from France

After four long, hard years of war, New Zealand servicemen were understandably keen to get back to the home they had fought for. The poem inside this card, redolent with imagery of the country they had not seen perhaps for years, encapsulates that sentiment:

*God gave all men all earth to love
But since our hearts are small
Ordained for each one spot should be
Beloved over all.
Gorse behind the windy town, pollen o' the pine
Bell-bird in the leafy deep where the Ratas twine
Ferns above the saddle-bow, flax upon the plain
'Tis where Pohutukawas bloom we long to be again.*

The card is addressed 'To Pater, With All Good Wishes, From Bob, somewhere in France' and is dated November 4, 1918 — just a week before the armistice was declared on November 11.

The front of the card bears the words 'Cheerio from France' and a drawing of a damaged windmill, labelled 'A diggers' landmark'. This is probably a windmill at Courcelles in northern France, which withstood repeated shelling and became a landmark for New Zealand troops fighting in the area. On the back is a drawing of a Salvation Army barracks, with the caption 'A "Diggers'" home, somewhere in France'.

As well as being called Anzacs, New Zealand and Australian troops had become known as 'diggers', possibly because of the command given to 'dig in' at Gallipoli, or because many of the soldiers had backgrounds as goldminers or gumdiggers.

*Cheerio from France. Christmas 1918. A "Diggers'" landmark / Johns. [Card].
Print, navy on white card,
folded to 143 x 115 mm
Eph-A-CARDS-Christmas-WWI-1918-03*

To Pater

With All Good Wishes

From Bob

Somewhere in France
4/11/18

"Somewhere in France."

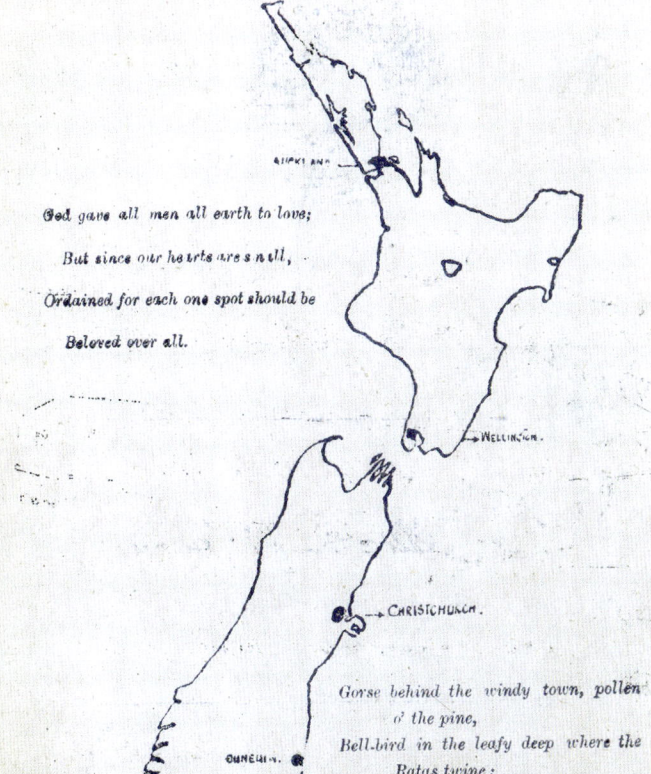

God gave all men all earth to love;
But since our hearts are small,
Ordained for each one spot should be
Beloved over all.

Gorse behind the windy town, pollen o' the pine,
Bell-bird in the leafy deep where the Ratas twine;
Fern above the saddle-bow, flax upon the plain,
'Tis where Pohutukawas bloom we long to be again.

1914–18
Christmas greetings from New Zealand — ake ake

During the four years of the First World War, few New Zealand families were untouched by the conflict. Christmas was a time of special reflection on the fate of family and friends, fighting half a world away in unimaginable conditions.

This card, produced by Frank Duncan and Co of Auckland, is redolent with New Zealand imagery, with a tiki, mere and maidenhair fern on the left and a flax bush, palisaded pa and steaming mountain on the right. The poem reads:

In my loneliness I ponder,
Think of you by night and day,
Of you bravely fighting yonder;
May God keep you safe I pray.

The words 'ake ake' mean 'forever and ever' and were used in the marching song of the Maori (28) Battalion in the Second World War.

As the First World War dragged on, the feeling at home in New Zealand moved from enthusiasm and patriotism to war-weariness and cynicism. While 14,000 men had enlisted in the first week after war broke out in 1914, by 1916 enlistment rates were falling and only 30 per cent of men eligible for military service had volunteered. Conscription for Pakeha males was introduced in August of that year, and for Maori in June 1917. Conscientious objection to service became a major issue, and large numbers of men were imprisoned and subjected to physical punishment in an attempt to change their minds. Around 2600 conscientious objectors were denied the right to vote for 10 years and barred from working in national or local government positions.

By the end of hostilities in 1918, more than 100,000 New Zealanders, including 30,000 conscripts, had been sent to war. Nearly 17,000 had been killed and 41,000 wounded — the highest casualty rate per head of population of any country in the British Empire.

Postcard. Christmas greetings from New Zealand. Published by Frank Duncan & Co., High St., Auckland [1914–1918]
From Album of postcards donated by the Hurley family, page 10.
Chromolithograph on postcard, 94 x 139 mm
Eph-B-POSTCARD-Vol-17-010-1

1917 and 1918
The 'digger' at Christmas

New Zealand had gone into the First World War without its own army and with only the beginnings of an independent national identity. However, four years of bloody battle later, Kiwi soldiers were well known as a force apart from the British.

One of the most distinctive features of the New Zealand soldiers was their lemon-squeezer hats, with a central peak surrounded by four indents. The lemon-squeezer is said to have been developed in 1911 by Lieutenant Colonel William Malone (see page 92); finding that the fore-and-aft dented hats his troop of Taranaki riflemen wore tended to collect rainwater in their central dent, he redesigned the hat so the water ran off more easily. When Malone was appointed to command the 1st Battalion of the 5th Wellington Regiment at the start of the First World War, his 'Wellingtons' adopted this style of hat, which was more widely distributed from mid-1916 to other troops. During the First World War the hats were mostly manufactured in England, and became a highly visible way to distinguish between the New Zealanders and other colonial troops.

The lemon-squeezer was dropped from the New Zealand Army uniform in 1962 but later reinstated, and now forms part of the army's Ceremonial 1A dress uniform, with a coloured band, known as a puggaree, denoting rank and division.

The card on the left dates from 1917 and was designed by New Zealand Division artist William Frederick Bell. It shows a Kiwi soldier resting on a milestone upon which is engraved 'France to New Zealand, 13,000 miles'. The card on the right is from 1918 and was designed by soldier and artist Lieutenant George Patrick (Pat) Hanna.

Bell, William Frederick, 1896–1920
Aotearoa. [Greetings card. 1917]
Photolithograph,
on folded card 180 x 135 mm
Eph-A-CARDS-Christmas-WWI-1917-01

'With every wish that's brightest & best',
GP Hanna.
N.Z. Division, France. Xmas 1918.
Photolithograph on card,
186 x 126 mm
Eph-A-WAR-WI-1918-02

1919
The Christmas spirit chases away gloom, malice and general selfishness

With the signing of the armistice in November 1918, a war-weary world prepared to return to something approaching normality and to celebrate its first peacetime Christmas for four years

This cartoon, from the January 1919 edition of the New Zealand Returned Soldiers' Association's newspaper *Quick March*, shows a cheerful crowd of children led by Santa Claus going 'over the top' to chase away the spectres of Gloom, Malice, General Selfishness and one called 'Grouch', which has fallen into the trench. The caption is forward-thinking:

> *In the New Year and in the New Era, 'Quick March' will keep you on side in Life's Battle. Try a year's course of this cure for pessimism and all pettiness of spirit.*

Quick March was published monthly by the association in Wellington from April 1918 to June 1923. Its first edition appeared on Anzac Day 1918, which just three years after the Gallipoli landings had already become a national day of commemoration, although it did not become a public holiday until 1921.

The RSA was established in 1916 by returned soldier Captain Donald Simson, who had been wounded at Gallipoli. By 1920 it had 57,000 members, about 70 per cent of the returned soldier population. However, its membership dropped away in the 1920s as soldiers were rehabilitated, and *Quick March* was replaced by the more modest *RSA Review*. The association's popularity rose again during the Depression of the 1930s and following the Second World War. Renamed the New Zealand Returned Services' Association, it had around 136,000 members by 1947.

Cartoonist unknown
The Christmas spirit chases away gloom, malice and gen. selfishness. Quick March, *January 1919.*
A-313-13-001

In the New Year and in the New Era "Quick March" will keep you on side in Life's Battle. Try a year's course of this cure for pessimism and all pettiness of spirit. Send 7/- to-day (for a year's copies, posted) to Manager, "Quick March," Box 1010, Wellington.

1921 • Thomas Ellis Glover
His Christmas dream

By Christmas 1921, the New Zealand economy had entered a period of difficulty, a flow-on effect from a depressed economy worldwide and low primary produce prices in the London markets. Many returned servicemen who had taken up grants of land were walking off their farms or facing severe economic hardship.

This cartoon, published in *The Free Lance* on December 21, 1921, makes fun of Prime Minister and Minister of Finance William Massey, a career politician who first entered the House in 1894. He was Prime Minister, leading Reform and National governments (the latter a wartime coalition with Liberal Joseph Ward) for nearly 13 years from 1912 until his death in office in May 1925. With the farming sector, Massey's traditional support base, shrinking as more people moved to the cities, the Reform party won the 1922 election only narrowly, and economic conditions continued to worsen.

In this cartoon, Massey is portrayed as the Christmas good fairy, offering a little boy representing New Zealand such goodies as 'war prices for wool', 'no debt', 'houses for all', 'no taxes' and 'cheap railway fares', and saying 'Help yourself little boy!'

The cartoon was drawn by Thomas Ellis Glover, known as Tom Glover when drawing for the *New Zealand Truth* newspaper and as Tom Ellis when moonlighting for *The Free Lance*. Glover's habit of drawing caricatures of passengers while working as an elevator boy led to his employment as a cartoonist at *New Zealand Truth* for 11 years. He moved to Australia to work for *The Sun* in Sydney in 1931, and died on the job in 1938. Many of the politicians he had lampooned through his work attended his funeral.

Glover, Thomas Ellis, 1891?–1938
His Christmas dream; the story of the Little Boy who dreamt that he spent Christmas Eve with William the Good Fairy. 1921.
In New Zealand Free Lance, *21 December 1921, front page*
PUBL-0096-1921-12-21-001

An Illustrated Journal of Information and Racy Comment upon Topics of the Hour.

22ND YEAR OF ISSUE—No. 25.　　WEDNESDAY, DECEMBER 21, 1921.　　EIGHTPENCE.

HIS CHRISTMAS DREAM.
The Story of the Little Boy who Dreamt that he spent Christmas Eve with William the Good Fairy.

1925
THE SLEEPING BEAUTY

By the 1920s, radio and cinema were beginning to surpass the theatre as New Zealand's principal source of entertainment, but the Christmas pantomime remained popular.

This 1925 production of 'an entirely new and modernised version' of *The Sleeping Beauty* was staged at the Theatre Royal Christchurch, written by Gwen Merrett and produced by Ngaio Marsh. The programme features a portrait of the young Marsh, aged 30.

Marsh had been brought up in Christchurch and attended classes part-time at the Canterbury College School of Art. She became interested in acting, and as well as writing several plays she toured the country with various companies. During the 1920s she produced several large-scale fundraising shows such as *The Sleeping Beauty* for Unlimited Charities, which raised money for the Nurse Maude District Nursing Association and the Plunket Society. During this period she became friendly with one of Canterbury's oldest landed families, the Rhodeses, through the association with Unlimited Charities of Captain Tahu Rhodes and his wife Helen.

It was not until a visit to England in 1928 to stay with the Rhodes–Plunket families that Marsh started to write the detective stories for which she would become famous. The first of these, *A Man Lay Dead*, was published in 1934; by her death in 1982 she had written 32, all featuring the detective Roderick Alleyn. In the 1940s she became involved with Canterbury University College's drama productions at the Little Theatre — described as a 'small but unmistakable Golden Age' of theatre — mostly directing Shakespearean productions.

This production of *The Sleeping Beauty*, in pantomime tradition, gave a contemporary twist to the fairy tale, with the play starting in England 'JBC' ('just before the Conqueror') and concluding in 1925 — giving the opportunity for the chorus to appear in modern, flapper-style dresses. It also included 'an address on the rearing of infants, given with special regard for the requirements of the Plunket nurses'.

Theatre Royal, Christchurch Unlimited Charities presents an entirely new and modernised version of 'The Sleeping Beauty'. Printed by Smith and Anthony, Ltd, Manchester Street, Christchurch. [Programme. 1925] Programme of 20 pages, 248 x 188 mm Eph-A-PANTOMIME-1925-01

1930s • ROBERT NETTLETON FIELD
NATIVITY SCENE

The scene of the Nativity is one of the most familiar of the Christmas story, with the baby Jesus in the arms of his mother. This modernist image of a traditional theme was painted in the 1930s by Robert Nettleton Field.

Field was an English-born artist and teacher brought to New Zealand under the La Trobe scheme, which in the 1920s and 1930s assisted art teachers to emigrate in the hope of improving the quality of tuition in technical colleges and art schools. Among them were Christopher Perkins and Roland Hipkins, who along with Field brought a breath of Modernist air to the New Zealand art scene.

Field, a painter and sculptor who had trained at London's Royal College of Art, settled in Dunedin in 1925 and started work at the Dunedin School of Art, teaching drawing, sculpture, outdoor sketching, life drawing, painting and linocut techniques. He cut a striking figure on the streets of Dunedin, and his Modernist paintings were considered challenging by many in the conservative art scene.

In the 1920s and 1930s Field painted mostly portraits, landscapes and still lifes in bright colours, as this image shows. One of his best-known works, *Christ at the Well of Samaria* (1929), was painted in situ on the servery door of his house, with the timber left bare to show the wood grain in some areas.

After a visit to Britain in 1932–33 he returned to New Zealand with a passion for studio pottery. In 1945 he became head of the art department at Auckland's Avondale College, where he set up this country's first ceramic training centre and taught such artists as Len Castle and Barry Brickell.

This gouache painting on a small card is part of a collection of portraits, bird and animal studies and scenes of Auckland, Canterbury and Otago, mostly from the 1920s and 1930s, which Field donated to the Alexander Turnbull Library in 1976.

Field, Robert Nettleton, 1899–1987
[Nativity scene. 1930s?]
Gouache, 190 x 120 mm
A-265-120
© RN Field Estate

Santa Claus at a Public Health Camp 1931
Photographer: Gordon Burt
Gordon Burt Collection
1/1-015745-F

57

1931 • Gordon Burt
Santa Claus promotes children's health camps

Concern over public health in general and the health of children in particular led to the issue of New Zealand's first fundraising stamps, promoted for use on Christmas mail.

The idea of issuing stamps to raise funds for charity came from Denmark, which issued 'Christmas seals' with a fundraising component from 1904. Danish immigrant Kirstine Nelson had seen the idea in action when visiting her homeland in the 1910s, and in the late 1920s approached Lady Fergusson, the wife of Governor-General Sir Bernard Fergusson, with the idea. The first issue, in 1929, bore the words 'help stamp out tuberculosis', but from this issue in 1931 funds were directed to the growing health-camp movement.

The first informal health camp was organised by Dr Elizabeth Gunn at Turakina, near Marton, in 1919. The movement spread around the country in the 1920s and 1930s, fuelled by contemporary ideals of breeding a healthy stock of young New Zealanders following the decimation of the First World War. In 1937 it became more formalised and controlled by the Department of Health, with permanent camps set up in the 1930s and 1940s at Otaki, Roxburgh in Central Otago, Maunu near Whangarei, Gisborne, Glenelg in Christchurch, and Bucklands Beach in Auckland.

The 1931 stamp issue was not a huge success, raising just £778 — adding an extra penny for charity, essentially doubling the price of the stamp, may have been too big a step for many in a depressed economy. Greater promotion was then put into the stamp issues, and by 1935–36 around £11,700 was raised through stamp sales and donations. Ironically, both the red and black versions of the 1931 stamp, known as the 'Smiling Boy', are now the rarest and most valuable of the health stamps.

Health stamps are still produced today, with an extra 10 cents added to the postage charge per stamp to raise funds for New Zealand's seven remaining children's health camps/Te Puna Whaiora.

1933 • AH and AW Reed
First New Zealand Christmases

'As generation succeeds generation, and Maoriland develops into a great nation, that thrice happy day will stand out with the same relative importance as does the landing of Augustine on the Isle of Thanet twelve centuries and more before.'

Writer and publisher Clif Reed's words may have been heartfelt, but 75 years later few people give a thought to the first Christian service delivered in New Zealand, on Christmas Day 1814. This little book, published by legendary New Zealand company AH and AW Reed, tells the story of 'the first New Zealand Christmases' — including visits to New Zealand around Christmas time by Abel Tasman and James Cook, but mostly paying tribute to the Reverend Samuel Marsden's first service, held at Rangihoua on the northern side of the Bay of Islands. Reed paints a moving picture of what that first service in the strange land may have been like:

> *From the bush and the trees that towered above rose a wondrous diapason of sound — the deep-toned organ of the New Zealand native bush in the summer time; the throbbing bass of innumerable insects, the soft sighing of the wind in the trees, and the lapping of the waves on the Oihi beach.*

A slim volume at just 24 pages, the book was published as part of a series of 'Raupo Readers' designed for use by teachers as a cheaper supplement to large textbooks. It was first published in October 1933 and reprinted straight away. As with many early Reed publications, it was printed by Coulls Somerville Wilkie, Dunedin.

First New Zealand Christmases was one of the first publications from the fledgling firm of AH and AW Reed, established by Alfred (AH) and his nephew Clif (AW) Reed in Dunedin in the early 1930s. The company went on to become one of the most significant in New Zealand publishing, and the local industry lamented its passing in late 2007 when, following in an international merger between parent companies it was taken over by Penguin.

Published in First New Zealand Christmases, *by AH and AW Reed (Dunedin: Reed, 1933)*
B-K 842-COVER
© Richards Literary Agency

MANUKA (LEPTOSPERMUM SCOPARIUM)

1934
Christmas shoppers' and gift givers' guide

Despite tough economic conditions in the early 1930s, this selection of Christchurch retailers was still hopeful of attracting plenty of shoppers at Christmas 1934.

First up in this 20-page advertising booklet is the perennial Christmas favourite: 'Bargains in Xmas Liquor from the Provincial Hotel, cnr Cashel and Barbadoes Sts'. As well as a range of beers, wines, and local and imported spirits, the Provincial offered a series of hampers, starting with a selection of a bottle of whisky, two bottles of port, three bottles of ale or stout and one small bottle of brandy for 20 shillings — the equivalent of about $150 nowadays. The Provincial also offered bottles of Speight's ale at 1/4.

Newfangled electrical gifts suggested by HC Urlwin Ltd, 'electragists', included toaster stoves, electric jugs and irons. Sports equipment retailers Ashby Bergh & Co also offered electrical goods such as soldering irons, electric safety kettles and 'the silent Silo-vac vacuum cleaner' for a staggering £14 — about $2000 in today's money. Costing a little more — £19 cash — was an all-electric radio in a Bakelite cabinet from Butlers.

For younger relatives, Ashby Bergh offered a range of Slazenger tennis racquets ranging in price from 37/6 to 95 shillings, as well as more affordable items such as air rifles, torches, tricycles and clockwork vans and trucks. For women, 'a special item of interest this year will be the Xylonite [plastic polymer] Toilet Ware in fancy shapes and choice colours', with brush sets from 20 to 100 shillings.

The double-page spread from department store Minsons exhorts buyers:

You cannot escape it — your friends are sure to remember you. What are you yourself doing about it? After all, Christmas only comes once a year and life is not much without friends, is it?

Minsons offered a range of china, dinner sets ('no longer a luxury — a necessity'), gifts for men such as pipes and razors, crystal, Sheffield ware and electrical goods, the result of '12 solid months of buying from England chiefly'. The advertisement concluded: 'No good putting our prices here. You are sure to be satisfied with them.'

Xmas shoppers' & gift givers' guide. Printed by Simpson & Williams Ltd., 169 St Asaph Street, Christchurch [1934?]
Booklet of 20 pages, each 240 x 180 mm
Eph-A-RETAIL-1934-01

1934
He awhina — a friendly wish

This Christmas card was sent following a trip to New Zealand in 1934 by a group of British schoolgirls, among them Rachel Mooring Aldridge. Rachel spent several weeks in the country, touring with a group of around 25 girls under the guidance of a Miss Thompson, seeing the sights and being billeted by local families.

Some highlights of the trip are revealed in a letter to Rachel's mother in England from Brownie Hassell of Wellington, who billeted Rachel. Mrs Hassell wrote to Mrs Aldridge on September 30, 1934 to report that Rachel and the other girls had had a busy but enjoyable trip, visiting Rotorua — 'one of the wonders of the world' — and the Waitomo Caves — 'the most beautiful thing in nature I have ever seen . . . quite unspoilt by man'. The party had also attended a lunch at Government House.

Mrs Hassell also recounts an 'amusing experience': Rachel had received a letter when her ship arrived in Wellington from a young man who said he came from Rachel's hometown of Bournemouth, 'saying that he had seen her name in the paper as coming from Bournemouth and he would very much like to show her a bit of New Zealand and send messages home'. Mrs Hassell took Rachel to visit him in Petone.

> *I thought possibly he was a homesick youth and wanted cheering up by the sight of someone from Home. Not at all: he was just an impudent creature who thought he could strike up an acquaintance with one of the English girls and boast to his friends.*

This card, sent to Rachel by a New Zealander she met on the trip, Jean Stevenson, has a cut-out on the front to reveal the 'Maori belles' inside, along with the words 'Nga Mihi o te Kirihimete me Nga Tumanako Papai Katoa mo te Tau Hou na (Christmas greetings and all good wishes for the New Year)'. Rachel Aldridge donated the letter and card to the Alexander Turnbull Library from her home in England in 2007.

He awhina! Translation – 'A friendly wish'. [Christmas greeting card from Jean Stevenson to Rachel Aldridge, ca 1934] Photolithograph, on card 150 x 104 mm Eph-A-CARDS-Christmas-1934-01

He awhina!

TRANSLATION:
"A Friendly Wish"

1934–35
Christmas and New Year holiday timetable

In the 1930s New Zealand's rail network was thriving, as this schedule of train and steamer services over the 1934–35 Christmas–New Year period shows.

While today just two regular passenger routes remain in the South Island — between Picton and Christchurch, and Christchurch and Greymouth — with a freight-only line between Christchurch, Dunedin and Invercargill, in the 1930s an active and extensive network of main trunk and branch lines connected the lower South Island.

The Christchurch–Dunedin section of the South Island main trunk railway opened in 1878, linking through to Invercargill in 1879. A network of numerous branch railways was also constructed, many in Canterbury and Southland, during the railway boom of the 1870s, and lines were built through the more difficult landscape of Central Otago in the 1890s and through to the First World War. The longest branch, the Otago Central Railway from Dunedin to Cromwell, was not completed until 1921. The trains are now long gone, but this section of what was once railway has now found new life as the Otago Central Rail Trail.

This schedule includes the Lake Wakatipu steamer service, from Kingston at the southern end of the lake to Queenstown. The boat service had been established as an alternative to the tortuous wagon road through the Kawarau Gorge from Cromwell. Kingston was 140 km from Invercargill and 280 km from Dunedin by rail, with a further 33 km journey up the lake to Queenstown on steamers such as the TSS *Earnslaw*, which came into service in 1912 and still plies the lake today.

However, in 1936 a road, built by unemployed relief workers, was opened from Kingston to Frankton and Queenstown along the foot of the Remarkables. In 1937 many rail passenger services to Kingston were replaced by buses that went right through to Queenstown. The Kingston railway line was finally fully closed in 1979, and is now the home of the vintage train the Kingston Flyer.

New Zealand Railways: Christmas and New Year holidays 1934–1935. Principal train arrangements and Lake Wakatipu steamer service. Coulls Somerville Wilkie Ltd., Printers, Dunedin, 1934. Lithograph, 920 x 590 mm
Eph-E-RAIL-1934-01

CHRISTMAS AND NEW YEAR HOLIDAYS 1934-1935

PRINCIPAL TRAIN ARRANGEMENTS AND LAKE WAKATIPU STEAMER SERVICE

EXPRESS and MAIL TRAINS

LYTTELTON-CHRISTCHURCH-DUNEDIN-INVERCARGILL

DAILY (except Sunday) from 19th December, 1934, until 4th February, 1935, inclusive.

		a.m.	a.m.	p.m.
CHRISTCHURCH	dep	...	ƒ8.35†	12.25
TIMARU	dep	...	11.33	3.46
OAMARU	dep	...	p.m. 1.19	5.49
DUNEDIN	arr	...	4.18	8.54
"	dep	8.33*	4.40	...
CLINTON	dep	11.11	7.7	...
INVERCARGILL	arr	p.m. 1.10	8.5	...

* On 22nd, 24th and 25th December, 1934, and 2nd January, 1935, leaves Dunedin 9.0 a.m., Clinton 11.39 a.m., Invercargill arrive 1.38 p.m.

† During the daily running of 8.35 a.m. Christchurch-Invercargill Express train the Mail train usually leaving Christchurch at 8.35 a.m. on MONDAYS for DUNEDIN (Dunedin arrive 5.1 p.m.) will NOT run.

		a.m.	a.m.	p.m.
INVERCARGILL	dep	...	ƒ7.0	1.45*
CLINTON	dep	...	9.7	3.55
DUNEDIN	arr	...	11.20	6.23
"	dep	8.40	11.35	...
OAMARU	dep	p.m. 12.8	p.m. 3.0	...
TIMARU	dep	1.54	4.34	...
CHRISTCHURCH	arr	5.10	7.26	...
" ...	dep	...	7.37	...
LYTTELTON WHARF ...	arr	...	7.56‡	...

‡ Connects with Steamer Express Service for Wellington.

* On 22nd, 24th and 25th December, 1934, and 2nd January, 1935, leaves Invercargill 2.5 p.m., Clinton 4.16, Dunedin arrive 6.53 p.m.

ƒ On Sunday, 23rd December, the 8.35 a.m. Christchurch-Invercargill Express train WILL run. The 7.0 a.m. Invercargill-Lyttelton Express train WILL run from Invercargill to CHRISTCHURCH only.

LYTTELTON LINE

From 19th December, 1934, to 4th February, 1935, the usual 8.40 p.m. TUESDAY, WEDNESDAY, THURSDAY, FRIDAY, SATURDAY Lyttelton-Christchurch train will run DAILY (except Sunday).

NOTE.—On Tuesday, 25th December, will leave Lyttelton at 8.35 p.m.

METHVEN BRANCH

From 1st January to 29th January the usual 3.0 p.m. Methven-Rakaia TUESDAY train will leave Methven 2.25 p.m., Rakaia arrive 3.55 p.m., connecting with the 8.40 a.m. Dunedin-Christchurch Mail train.

On MONDAY, 24th December, Special train will leave Rakaia for Methven at 10.10 a.m. after arrival of the 9.10 a.m. Relief Express from Christchurch.

On MONDAY, 31st December, Special train will leave Rakaia for Methven at 9.40 a.m. after arrival of the 8.35 a.m. Express from Christchurch.

On MONDAY, 24th December, and MONDAY, 31st December, Special train will leave Methven 2.40 p.m., Rakaia arrive 3.55 p.m., connecting with the 8.40 a.m. Dunedin-Christchurch Mail train.

WAIMATE BRANCH

From 19th December, 1934, to 4th February, 1935, inclusive (except Sundays), buses will run DAILY to connect at Studholme with ordinary Down and Up Express and Mail trains.

		a.m.	p.m.	p.m.	p.m.
WAIMATE	dep	11.35	12.35	3.10	4.10
WAIMATE POST OFFICE	"	11.40	12.38	3.15	4.13
STUDHOLME	arr	12.0	12.58	3.35	4.33

		p.m.	p.m.	p.m.	p.m.
STUDHOLME	dep	12.12	1.9	3.46	4.43
WAIMATE	arr	12.32	1.29	4.6	5.3

On Sunday, 23rd December, buses connect at Studholme with 8.35 a.m. Christchurch-Invercargill, and 7.0 a.m. Invercargill-Christchurch Express trains.

OAMARU-DUNEDIN

From 20th December, 1934, to 4th February, 1935, the 4.25 p.m., Oamaru-Palmerston train usually leaving Hampden at 6.8 p.m. on Monday, Tuesday, Thursday and Saturday will leave Hampden at 7.8 p.m. DAILY (except Saturday and Sunday), Palmerston arrive 8.15 p.m.

On SATURDAYS trains leaves Hampden 6.51 p.m., Palmerston arrive 7.56 p.m.

ROXBURGH BRANCH

On Saturday, 22nd, and Monday, 24th December, 1934, usual 6.40 p.m. Milton-Lawrence train will leave Milton at 7.5 p.m., Lawrence arrive 8.49 p.m. Connects at Milton with 4.48 p.m. and 5.43 p.m. trains from Dunedin.

On Tuesday, 25th December, 1934, trains leave Lawrence for Milton at 8.10 a.m., Milton for Roxburgh at 10.29 a.m., and Roxburgh for Lawrence at 2.45 p.m.

CATLINS RIVER BRANCH

On Saturday, 22nd December, 1934, trains leave Balclutha for Tahakopa at 10.55 a.m. and Tahakopa for Balclutha at 11.55 a.m., connecting with Down and Up Mail trains respectively. Special train leaves Balclutha for Owaka at 7.35 p.m., connecting with 5.43 p.m. Relief Express train from Dunedin.

On Monday, 24th December, 1934, the usual 10.30 a.m. Balclutha-Tahakopa and 11.30 a.m. Tahakopa-Balclutha trains will NOT run.

Special train, connecting with Down Mail trains and 9.30 a.m. Special passenger train from Dunedin, leaves Balclutha for Tahakopa at 11.55 a.m. Special train leaves Tahakopa at 11.30 a.m., Balclutha arrive 3.7 p.m., connecting with Special train leaving Balclutha for Dunedin at 3.20 p.m.

Special train leaves Balclutha for Tahakopa at 9.28 p.m., connecting with 6.40 p.m. Invercargill-Christchurch Express train and 7.0 p.m. Dunedin-Balclutha special passenger train.

On Tuesday, 25th December, 1934, the 6.40 a.m. Tahakopa-Balclutha and 6.30 p.m. Balclutha-Tahakopa trains will NOT run.

Special train leaves Balclutha for Tahakopa at 10.55 a.m., connecting with Down Mail trains from Dunedin. Special train leaves Tahakopa at 2.5 p.m., Balclutha arrive 4.50 p.m., connecting with 4.57 p.m. Up Relief Mail train for Dunedin.

On Wednesday, 2nd January, 1935, trains leave Balclutha for Tahakopa at 10.55 a.m. and Tahakopa for Balclutha at 11.55 a.m., connecting with Down and Up Mail trains respectively.

TAPANUI BRANCH

From THURSDAY, 20th December, 1934, to SATURDAY, 5th January, 1935, the usual timetable for the Edievale-Waipahi Road Motor Service will be suspended, and Road Motor Services will run as follows:—

TO WAIPAHI	1 Daily except Sun. and Dec. 25 and 31 and Jan. 1	2 Monday Dec. 31	3 Tuesday, Jan. 1	4 Dec. 20, 22, 24, 26, 27 and 29, and Jan. 1, 2, 3, and 5
	a.m.	a.m.	a.m.	p.m.
EDIEVALE dep	6.30	9.0	8.5	5.15
WAIPAHI arr	8.25	10.55	10.0	7.10

FROM WAIPAHI	5 Daily except Sun. and Dec. 22, 24 and 25, and Jan. 2	6 Dec. 22 and 24 and Jan. 2	7 Dec. 20, 22, 24, 26, 27 and 29 and Jan. 1, 2, 3 and 5
	a.m.	p.m.	p.m.
WAIPAHI dep	11.45	12.15	7.40
EDIEVALE arr	1.40	2.10	9.35

1. Connects with 7.0 a.m. Invercargill-Lyttelton Express.
2. Connects with 8.33 a.m. Dunedin-Invercargill Mail train.
3. Connects with 7.30 a.m. Dunedin-Wyndham Special Race train.
4. Connects with 8.35 a.m. Christchurch-Invercargill Express.
5. Connects with 8.33 a.m. Dunedin-Invercargill Mail train.
6. Connects with 8.33 a.m. Dunedin-Gore and 9.0 a.m. Dunedin-Invercargill Mail trains.
7. Connects with 8.35 a.m. Christchurch-Invercargill Express, and on 26th December and 1st January with Special trains from Gore and Wyndham Races.

TRAIN SERVICE, TAPANUI BRANCH.—On SATURDAY, 22nd December, 1934, special train for Waipahi leaves Edievale 6.45 a.m., Heriot 7.10, Tapanui 7.40, Waipahi arrive 8.25 a.m. Connects at Waipahi with 7.0 a.m. Invercargill-Lyttelton Express.

On SATURDAY and MONDAY, 22nd and 24th December, 1935, special train (connecting at Waipahi with 4.40 p.m. Dunedin-Invercargill Express) will leave Waipahi 7.30 p.m., Tapanui 8.15, Heriot 8.53, Edievale arrive 9.18 p.m.

DUNEDIN-INVERCARGILL-QUEENSTOWN

(VIA WAIMEA PLAINS BRANCH)

DAILY (except Sunday) from 19th December, 1934, until 4th February, 1935, inclusive.

		a.m.	a.m.
DUNEDIN	dep	...	8.33
INVERCARGILL	dep	*10.25	...
GORE	arr	p.m. 12.36	11.57
GORE	dep		p.m. 12.45
LUMSDEN	dep		2.37
KINGSTON (Steamer) ...	dep		4.30
QUEENSTOWN	arr		6.45

* Not 26th December.
* Not 1st January.

		a.m.	
QUEENSTOWN (Steamer) ...	dep	8.25	
KINGSTON (Rail)	dep	11.5	
LUMSDEN	dep	p.m. 1.4	
GORE	arr	2.35	
GORE	dep	p.m. 3.5	p.m. 2.59
INVERCARGILL	arr	5.18	...
DUNEDIN	arr	...	6.23

On 26th December train leaves Invercargill 10.5 a.m., Gore arrive 11.21 a.m.
On 1st January train leaves Invercargill 10.0 a.m., Gore arrive 12.35 p.m.

INVERCARGILL-CLINTON

From 19th December, 1934, to 4th February, 1935, the usual 6.50 a.m. Invercargill-Clinton MONDAY train will NOT run.

On Mondays, 24th and 31st December, 1934, 7th, 14th, 21st and 28th January and 4th February, 1935, this train will leave Invercargill at 6.10 a.m.

Goods Traffic will be suspended and Goods Sheds closed on 25th and 26th December, 1934, and 1st and 2nd January, 1935.

CHRISTCHURCH-ARTHURS PASS-GREYMOUTH

DAILY (except Sunday), from 18th December, 1934, to 5th January, 1935, inclusive.
and on MONDAY, TUESDAY, THURSDAY and SATURDAY, from 7th January, to 5th February, 1935, inclusive.

		a.m.
CHRISTCHURCH	dep	10.0
SPRINGFIELD	dep	11.33
OTIRA	dep	p.m. 2.29
GREYMOUTH	arr	4.29

		a.m.
GREYMOUTH	dep	10.18
OTIRA	dep	p.m. 1.6
SPRINGFIELD	dep	3.38
CHRISTCHURCH	arr	5.0

On 22nd and 24th December, 1934, and 5th January, 1935, Relief Mail trains will leave Christchurch for Greymouth at 9.30 a.m. and Greymouth for Christchurch at 9.10 a.m.

On 24th December, 1934, passenger trains will leave Christchurch for Greymouth at 10.15 p.m., and Greymouth for Christchurch at 10.50 p.m.

NIGHT EXPRESS TRAINS

CHRISTCHURCH-DUNEDIN-INVERCARGILL

		SUNDAY p.m.
CHRISTCHURCH ...	dep	11.2
		MONDAY a.m.
TIMARU	dep	2.2
OAMARU	dep	3.40
DUNEDIN	arr	6.53

Connects at Dunedin with 8.33 a.m. Mail train for Invercargill, except on Monday, 24th December, when a connection will be made with 9.0 a.m. Relief Mail train for Invercargill.

		SUNDAY p.m.
INVERCARGILL ...	dep	6.40
DUNEDIN	arr	10.57
"	dep	11.20
		MONDAY a.m.
OAMARU	dep	2.35
TIMARU	dep	4.18
CHRISTCHURCH ...	arr	7.18

RELIEF EXPRESS AND MAIL TRAINS

CHRISTCHURCH-DUNEDIN

		Dec. 21, 22, 24, 25, 26 and Jan. 2 and 5	Dec. 24
		a.m.	p.m.
CHRISTCHURCH	dep	9.10	12.45
TIMARU	"	p.m. 12.5	4.27
OAMARU	"	1.55	6.27
DUNEDIN	arr	5.1	9.32

DUNEDIN-CHRISTCHURCH

		Dec. 21, 22, 26, and Jan. 5	Dec. 24 and 25	Dec. 24	Jan. 2
		a.m.	a.m.	p.m.	p.m.
DUNEDIN	dep	10.47	9.5	12.5	1.30
OAMARU	"	p.m. 2.21	p.m. 12.37	3.31	4.56
TIMARU	"	3.57	2.31	5.14	6.43
CHRISTCHCH.	arr	7.12	5.55	8.6	9.33

CHRISTCHURCH-INVERCARGILL

22nd and 24th DECEMBER

		a.m.
CHRISTCHURCH	dep	9.10
TIMARU	"	p.m. 12.5
OAMARU	"	1.55
DUNEDIN	"	5.43
CLINTON	"	8.9
INVERCARGILL	arr	10.5

DUNEDIN-GORE

22nd, 24th, 25th DECEMBER and 2nd JANUARY

		a.m.
DUNEDIN	dep	8.33
CLINTON	dep	11.11
GORE ...	arr	11.57

		p.m.
GORE ...	dep	2.59
CLINTON	dep	3.55
DUNEDIN	arr	6.23

On the above dates the Down Mail Train leaves Dunedin at 9.0 a.m., Invercargill arr 1.38 p.m., and Up Mail leaves Invercargill 2.5 p.m., Dunedin arr 6.53 p.m.

DUNEDIN-INVERCARGILL

		Dec. 22	Dec. 22 and 24	Dec. 26
		p.m.	p.m.	a.m.
DUNEDIN ...	dep	1.35	5.43	7.45
BALCLUTHA	arr	3.12	7.23	9.35
"	dep	3.15	7.26	9.41
CLINTON ...	"	4.10	8.9	10.27
GORE ...	"	5.0	8.58	11.22
GORE RACECOURSE	arr	....	....	11.28
INVERCARGILL	arr	6.7	10.5	....

		Dec. 24	Dec. 26	Jan. 2
		p.m.	p.m.	p.m.
INVERCARGILL	dep	*6.40	....	6.40
GORE	"	7.55	6.55	7.55
CLINTON	"	8.53	7.50	8.47
BALCLUTHA	"	9.29	8.30	9.23
MILTON	"	10.4	9.6	9.58
DUNEDIN	arr	11.3	10.7	10.57

* Connects at Dunedin with 11.20 p.m. Dunedin-Christchurch Special Night Train

SPECIAL NIGHT TRAINS

CHRISTCHURCH-DUNEDIN-INVERCARGILL

		Express, Dec. 22	Dec. 24	Dec. 24	Dec. 24, Jan. 1
		p.m.	p.m.	p.m.	p.m.
CHRISTCHURCH	dep	11.2	9.28	10.25	...
		a.m. 23rd	a.m. 25th	a.m. 25th	
TIMARU ...	"	2.2	12.53	1.50	...
OAMARU ...	"	3.40	2.41	3.34	...
DUNEDIN ...	arr	6.53	6.0	6.53	...
" ...	dep	....	...	....	11.10
					a.m. 25th Dec. and 3rd January
CLINTON ...	"	....	...	....	2.14
INVERCARGILL ...	arr	...	...	...	4.46
		Bus to and from Waimate connects at Studholme	Bus to and from Waimate connects at Studholme	Bus to and from Waimate connects at Studholme	

		Express Dec. 22 and 24	Dec. 24
		p.m.	p.m.
DUNEDIN	dep	11.20	10.0
		a.m. Dec. 23 and 25	a.m. 25th
OAMARU	"	2.35	1.38
TIMARU	"	4.18	3.36
CHRISTCHURCH	arr	7.18	7.12
		Bus to and from Waimate connects at Studholme	Bus to and from Waimate connects at Studholme

LAKE WAKATIPU STEAMER SERVICE

QUEENSTOWN-KINGSTON.—From Wednesday, 19th December, 1934, to Saturday, 2nd February, 1935, inclusive, steamer will leave Queenstown for Kingston daily (except Sundays) at 8.25 a.m., returning leaving Kingston at 4.30 p.m.

From and including Monday, 4th February, the steamer between Queenstown and Kingston will revert to the ordinary running.

QUEENSTOWN—HEAD OF LAKE.

From Monday, 17th December, 1934, to Friday, 1st February, 1935, inclusive, steamer will run from Queenstown to Head of Lake as under:—

DAY EXCURSIONS.	ORDINARY TRIPS.	
MONDAY, 31st DECEMBER	MONDAY, 17th DECEMBER	WEDNESDAY, 9th JANUARY
MONDAY, 7th JANUARY	WEDNESDAY, 19th DECEMBER	FRIDAY, 11th JANUARY
TUESDAY, 15th JANUARY	FRIDAY, 21st DECEMBER	WEDNESDAY, 16th JANUARY
MONDAY, 21st JANUARY	MONDAY, 24th DECEMBER	FRIDAY, 18th JANUARY
MONDAY, 28th JANUARY	WEDNESDAY, 26th DECEMBER	WEDNESDAY, 23rd JANUARY
	FRIDAY, 28th DECEMBER	FRIDAY, 25th JANUARY
	WEDNESDAY, 2nd JANUARY	WEDNESDAY, 30th JANUARY
	FRIDAY, 4th JANUARY	FRIDAY, 1st FEBRUARY

From Monday, 4th Februray, 1935, and each succeeding Monday and Thursday, until further notice, steamer will run from Queenstown to Head of Lake.

DAY EXCURSION TICKETS will be issuable from Queenstown to Elfin Bay and Glenorchy from WEDNESDAY, 26th DECEMBER, 1934, until further notice.

Steamer leaves Queenstown at 8.30 a.m. and returns leaving Glenorchy at 4.0 p.m.

For particulars of Christmas Day train service, Mail, Express and Relief Express train arrangements and Branch Line connecting services for Christmas and New Year Holidays see Free Booklet obtainable at any Railway Station.

BY ORDER.

District Traffic Manager's Office,
Dunedin, 2nd November, 1934.

Coulls Somerville Wilkie Ltd., Printers, Dunedin.

CA 1935 • LEONARD MITCHELL
NEW ZEALAND TOURIST BROCHURE

This idyllic summer scene of a woman fly-fishing beneath a bough of rata was designed to attract tourists to this distant little country at the bottom of the world, where the seasons are reversed and Christmas falls in summertime.

'For entirely new and novel experiences in a land of brilliant sunshine, rich in natural wonders unsurpassed elsewhere in the world, visit New Zealand, the "Scenic Playground of the Pacific"', offers this brochure, produced by the government's Tourist and Publicity Department. 'Of special significance to the people of the Northern Hemisphere is the fact that in New Zealand their winter months are turned to summer, so that by visiting the Dominion they are able to escape the rigorous conditions prevailing in their own countries.'

The brochure extols the virtues of New Zealand's tourist attractions, as well as lauding an economy based on primary produce: chilled and frozen beef, mutton and lamb, butter, cheese and wool. It describes the country's main resorts such as the government spa at Rotorua, the Chateau Tongariro (see page 136) and the Hermitage (see page 188), and the new Milford Road, soon to provide road access to Milford Sound for the first time. It is illustrated with black-and-white photographs and colourful, poster-style images by Leonard Cornwall Mitchell, a commercial artist and stamp designer who designed posters and illustrations for Tourist and Publicity in the 1930s.

New Zealand was the first country in the world to set up a government tourist department, in 1901, to establish a chain of resorts and promote them internationally. In the 1938–39 season, the number of overseas tourists coming to New Zealand reached 20,000 for the first time; 60 per cent were from Australia.

Mitchell, Leonard Cornwall 1901–1971
New Zealand [Woman fishing. Cover. ca 1935]
Photolithograph 213 x 134 mm
Eph-A-TOURISM-NZ-1935-01-cover

1935 • DAVID LOW
SANTA CLAUS COMES TO MUSSOLINI

By Christmas 1935, war clouds were once again gathering in Europe. This cartoon by expatriate New Zealander David Low, published in the British newspaper *The Evening Standard*, satirises Italian dictator Benito Mussolini's invasion of Ethiopia.

Mussolini, who had dreams of establishing a new Italian empire to rival that of Rome, ordered the invasion of Ethiopia in October 1935, moving in from Italian-held Somaliland. After some fighting, Italy annexed Ethiopia in May 1936 and made it part of Italian East Africa, along with Somaliland and Eritrea. The skirmish was notable for the lack of action on the part of the newly formed League of Nations, the precursor to the United Nations, mainly because Britain and France were reluctant to impose sanctions such as oil restrictions on Italy, in the hope of keeping the country onside in the face of increasing German aggression.

Low's cartoon shows the dictator Mussolini asleep in bed, with the motto 'Violence on earth and the Devil take the hindmost' replacing the traditional Christmas 'Peace on earth and goodwill to all men'. An evil-looking Santa Claus is delivering him the emperor of Ethiopia, Haile Selassie, bound and gagged, while Santa's sleigh containing oil and the incapacitated League of Nations is being pulled by caricatures of European leaders.

Low, who was born in Dunedin in 1891, was one of the foremost cartoonists of his generation. His caricatures of Mussolini, Hitler and the stereotypical Colonel Blimp became classics during the European fascist era of the 1930s and the Second World War. Largely self-taught, Low worked as an artist and cartoonist in Christchurch when still in his teens, then moved to work in Australia. In 1919 he moved to London and contributed to the *Star*, the *Daily News*, *Punch* and then *The Evening Standard*, where he was resident cartoonist for 23 years. Because of his ridiculing of the European dictators, papers carrying his cartoons were banned in Germany from 1933 and Italy from 1935.

Low, David Alexander Cecil, 1891–1963. Santa Claus comes to Mussolini. Violence on earth and the Devil take the hindmost! [13 December 1935]
Pencil, ink, crayon, 349 x 524 mm (sheet size)
NON-ATL-C-0109
© David Low

1936 • Pat Lawlor
Murphy's Moa and other Xmas sketches

Stories lampooning the Christmas season, such as 'Murphy's Moa', 'The Degeneration of Santa Claus', 'Xmas in Hell' and 'The Tram Tragedy', are indicative of Wellington journalist Pat Lawlor's satirical eye and sense of humour.

This small book of humorous short stories, with illustrations by Gordon Minhinnick and Fred Alexander, was published by Christchurch printers and stationers Simpson and Williams in 1936. With the local publishing industry still in its infancy, the book's blurb proudly states that '*Murphy's Moa* is an all New Zealand production — author, subject matter, drawings and publisher, are all of this country'.

In his introduction, Lawlor notes that 'many writers are so sad and dreary when they write of Christmas'. His stories aimed to do away with traditions such as blazing Yule logs and hot puddings:

> *I have striven to make a clear break from the old Xmas idea . . . At all times I have tried to be gay and if I succeed in adding a few healthy laughs to this time of gladness, then surely I have done one good deed this year.*

Lawlor was a journalist and book collector, amassing a collection of around 12,000 New Zealand books as well as the signatures and papers of many well-known writers. He was a prolific author himself, writing more than 40 books and pamphlets, and is probably best known for his autobiographical works about Wellington in the first half of the twentieth century. Lawlor set up the New Zealand centre of the international writers' organisation PEN (now the New Zealand Society of Authors) in 1934 and helped to found the Friends of the Turnbull Library, to which he donated many of his papers in the 1970s.

Published in Murphy's moa and other Xmas sketches, *by Pat Lawlor (Christchurch: Simpson & Williams, 1936)*
B-K 841-COVER

1936 AND 1937
CHRISTMAS MENUS, CHATEAU TONGARIRO

These Christmas dinner menus from the Chateau Tongariro radiate an aura of luxury and grandeur, the sense of a resort hotel offering a luxury experience amid a dramatic landscape. In fact, the first 10 years of the Chateau's existence were fraught with financial problems, construction woes and illegal liquor scandals.

The hotel was built on land in Tongariro National Park, gifted to the state in 1887 by Ngati Tuwharetoa chief Te Heu Heu Tukino. In the 1920s the government became keen to develop and promote the park as a tourist attraction, and South Island tourism entrepreneur Rodolph Wigley won the concession to develop a hotel on the western side of Mount Ruapehu. The Chateau was conceived as a northern counterpart to The Hermitage at Mount Cook (see page 188), and replaced a draughty hut built at Whakapapa in 1921.

The hasty construction of the Chateau Tongariro began in February 1929, and a team of 180 men worked long hours to get it ready for the snow-sports season. In August that year competitors in the New Zealand national skiing championships stayed there in unfurnished rooms, and the official opening was held in November.

The hotel was the grandest in the country, with 90 bedrooms and 45 bathrooms, as well as a 464 sq m lounge and a dining room for 300 people. However, within 15 months the Chateau was in financial trouble, with Wigley going into liquidation in February 1931. The hotel passed into the hands of the government's tourist department, which cut costs and tried to promote the hotel. However, while more visitors were attracted, there was trouble with guests and staff smuggling alcohol into the hotel (the King Country area was dry at the time). The building also had serious structural issues, with a damaged roof, shonky foundations and numerous leaks. The hotel's fortunes were boosted in 1938, however, when Austrian instructor Ernst Skardarasy established a ski school based at the Chateau, and today it remains one of this country's iconic hotels.

Chateau Tongariro; The 'Chateau Tongariro', National Park, New Zealand. Dinner menus, Christmas 1936 and 1937. Photolithograph, on folded card 177 x 115 mm and photolithograph, 180 x 114 mm Eph-A-HOTEL-Tongariro-1936-01 and Eph-A-HOTEL-Tongariro-1937-01

Christmas, 1936.

The "Chateau Tongariro," National Park, New Zealand.

Dinner Menu.

Christmas 1937.

The "Chateau Tongariro," NATIONAL PARK, NEW ZEALAND.

DINNER MENU

1938
ATTRACTIONS AT THE EVANS BAY XMAS CARNIVAL

For a decade from the early 1930s to the early 1940s, one of Wellington's biggest Christmas attractions was the Evans Bay Christmas Carnival, organised by the Wellington Municipal Tramways Board.

Among the bizarre acts and freak shows that thrilled young and old were Anna John Budd — 'nature's greatest enigma' — and Chang the Pinhead Chinaman and a 'troup of clever Chinese'. We can only imagine how Budd might have appeared and speculate whether she was really a man or a woman, but show publicity describes her as:

> born a weakling, now a strong man . . . Direct from Canada. Part man, part woman — not an illusion. From one side, this remarkable person presents the perfect profile of a normally developed man, and the other gives the aspect of a well-proportioned female. Doctors and scientists are baffled — he or she?

She was in good company with Chang, touted as the smallest man alive, and with a head the size of an orange.

Many of the unusual attractions at the Evans Bay Carnival, including Budd and Chang, were brought to New Zealand by Sydney showman Arthur Greenhalgh and his business partner, Texan Ernest 'Jack' Jackson, who travelled the world to source bizarre acts. Highlights of the carnival over the years included the Headless Woman from Patagonia, 'viewed by over 40,000 at the Sydney Royal Show'; Princess Pontus, 'the last of the Amazon headhunters', purportedly 2.54 m tall and weighing 304 kg; Isom, the African pygmy said to be 90 cm high; and the world's smallest woman, Dollita, '20 years of age and 28 in [70 cm] high'. Other unusual offerings were Marjorie van Camp's original American Pig-a-Dilly Circus — 'six REAL live pigs who jump hurdles, ring bells, shoot guns off and stage a two-round fight in a miniature boxing arena' — American skaters Rex and Roma Roff, and Dennis O'Duffy, the giant Irish guardsman.

As well as the international 'acts', the annual carnival featured the usual rides and sideshows, a Bathing Beauty contest, regattas and speedboat races, and one year a confetti battle at midnight.

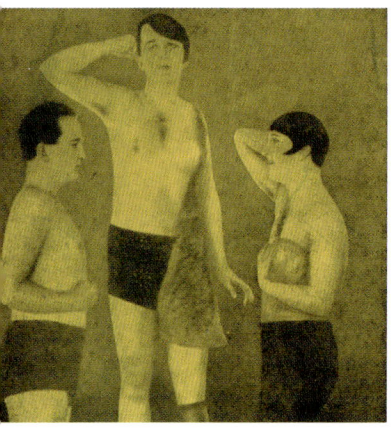

Evans Bay Xmas Carnival. Anna John Budd, woman turning into man. Nature's greatest enigma. See the double bodied personality star. A Greenhalgh & Jackson attraction [December 1938]; and Chang the pinhead Chinaman. See the man with the head the size of an orange, and Troup of clever Chinese. A Greenhalgh & Jackson attraction.
Photolithograph on yellow card, 252 x 316 mm and letterpress on yellow card, 242 x 312 mm
Eph-B-CABOT-Variety-1938-01 and Eph-B-CABOT-Variety-1938-02

EVANS BAY XMAS CARNIVAL

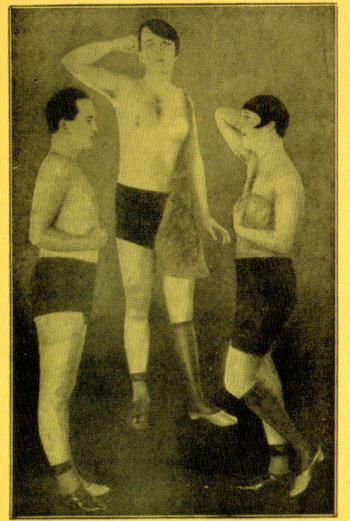

Anna John Budd

ANNA JOHN BUDD

Woman Turning to Man

NATURE'S GREATEST ENIGMA

SEE The Double Bodied Personality Star

A Greenhalgh & Jackson Attraction

EVANS BAY XMAS CARNIVAL

CHANG

THE PINHEAD CHINAMAN

See the Man with the Head the Size of an Orange

and

TROUP OF CLEVER CHINESE

● **A GREENHALGH AND JACKSON ATTRACTION**

CHRISTCHURCH PRESS

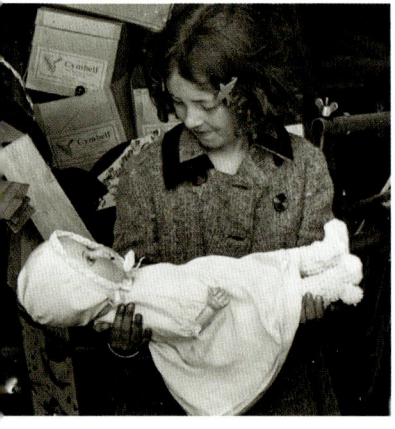

1938 • BERT SNOWDEN
HARRY WALMSLEY'S TOY HOSPITAL

Today, cheap plastic toys, often made in China, are usually thrown away when broken rather than sent to a 'hospital' for repairs. But Christmas 1938 was made a little brighter for some Auckland children through the repair work of Harry Walmsley.

This picture of Walmsley at work in his toy hospital, cigarette in mouth, was featured in the November 9 edition of the *New Zealand Free Lance*. A note on the back of the photograph reads 'Toys for Christmas: Damaged toys from warehouses are given to Mr Walmsley of Eastern Beach (Auckland) who repairs them and they are given to kindergartens, orphanages etc for distribution amongst the children'.

For many children brought up during the 'waste not, want not' years of the 1930s, starting with the Depression and ending in war, even a repaired toy would have been a welcome gift. By 1938, however, New Zealand's economy was on the mend, after spiralling downwards from the late 1920s and bottoming out in 1933, by which time around 80,000 people — about 12 per cent of the country's mostly male workforce — were unemployed and thousands of men were diverted into large-scale relief schemes and public works.

The tide turned in the mid-1930s with a recovery in international export prices. New Zealand's first Labour government, led by Michael Joseph Savage, swept to power in 1935, and was returned with an even larger majority in November 1938. After years of hardship, Labour's Social Security Act of 1938 brought in a free and universal health service and national superannuation from the age of 60, along with increases in benefits and pensions. But in less than a year's time New Zealand would again be at war.

James Robert Snowden (1904–1982)
Harry Walmsley's toy hospital, 1938
Photograph by Bert Snowden
New Zealand Free Lance Collection
PA7-21-42

1941
VICTORY 1942 CALENDAR

By Christmas 1941 New Zealand was at war again, following Germany's invasion of Poland in September 1939. The First Echelon of 6600 New Zealand troops left for training camps in the Middle East in January 1940, and by March 1941 soldiers began moving out from camp in Egypt into their first action of the Second World War.

The New Zealand forces, led by Major-General Bernard Freyberg, who had won the Victoria Cross in the First World War, were sent to Greece, but were quickly repelled by the invading Germans. When Greece capitulated they were forced to retreat to the island of Crete, with about 1600 New Zealanders taken prisoner in Greece and a further 2200 in Crete. New Zealanders were also engaged in combat in the North African desert. By Christmas 1941, another threat had become frighteningly real: on December 7, 1941 the Japanese bombed Pearl Harbor, bringing the United States into the war and focusing attention on Japanese aggression in the Pacific. While optimistic, with hindsight it seemed unlikely that there would indeed be victory in 1942.

This poster was produced by the RSA (see page 112) from a scroll received by soldiers in the Middle East. In the centre is the New Zealand Expeditionary Force's 1941 Christmas card, drawn by war artist Peter McIntyre. Arrayed around the V for Victory are the British royal family — King George VI and Queen Elizabeth, with the young princesses Elizabeth and Margaret, aged 15 and 11 respectively — as well as British Prime Minister Winston Churchill; Lieutenant-General Sir Alan Gordon Cunningham, commander of the British forces in North Africa, and his brother Admiral Sir Andrew Browne Cunningham, commander-in-chief of the Royal Navy's Mediterranean fleet; and Wing-Commander Arthur Coningham, commander of the Western Desert Air Force between 1941 and 1943. New Zealand's military leadership is represented by Freyberg (on the far right), and its forces by the signatures of members of various sections and battalions.

Victory 1942 calendar. Greetings from the N.Z.E.F. / reproduced by kind permission of Reg H Stillwell from the original scroll received from the Middle East [1942]. Photolithograph on poster 584 x 394 mm
Eph-D-WAR-WII-1941-01

Victory 1942

Greetings from the N.Z.E.F.

	JANUARY	FEBRUARY	MARCH	APRIL	MAY	JUNE
SUN.	4 11 18 25	1 8 15 22	1 8 15 22 29	5 12 19 26	3 10 17 24 31	7 14 21 28
Mon.	5 12 19 26	2 9 16 23	2 9 16 23 30	6 13 20 27	4 11 18 25	1 8 15 22 29
Tues.	6 13 20 27	3 10 17 24	3 10 17 24 31	7 14 21 28	5 12 19 26	2 9 16 23 30
Wed.	7 14 21 28	4 11 18 25	4 11 18 25	1 8 15 22 29	6 13 20 27	3 10 17 24
Thur.	1 8 15 22 29	5 12 19 26	5 12 19 26	2 9 16 23 30	7 14 21 28	4 11 18 25
Fri.	2 9 16 23 30	6 13 20 27	6 13 20 27	3 10 17 24	1 8 15 22 29	5 12 19 26
Sat.	3 10 17 24 31	7 14 21 28	7 14 21 28	4 11 18 25	2 9 16 23 30	6 13 20 27

	JULY	AUGUST	SEPTEMBER	OCTOBER	NOVEMBER	DECEMBER
SUN.	5 12 19 26	2 9 16 23 30	6 13 20 27	4 11 18 25	1 8 15 22 29	6 13 20 27
Mon.	6 13 20 27	3 10 17 24 31	7 14 21 28	5 12 19 26	2 9 16 23 30	7 14 21 28
Tues.	7 14 21 28	4 11 18 25	1 8 15 22 29	6 13 20 27	3 10 17 24	1 8 15 22 29
Wed.	1 8 15 22 29	5 12 19 26	2 9 16 23 30	7 14 21 28	4 11 18 25	2 9 16 23 30
Thur.	2 9 16 23 30	6 13 20 27	3 10 17 24	1 8 15 22 29	5 12 19 26	3 10 17 24 31
Fri.	3 10 17 24 31	7 14 21 28	4 11 18 25	2 9 16 23 30	6 13 20 27	4 11 18 25
Sat.	4 11 18 25	1 8 15 22 29	5 12 19 26	3 10 17 24 31	7 14 21 28	5 12 19 26

This Calendar is an acknowledgment of a contribution to the R.S.A. Appeal.
Reproduced by kind permission of Reg. H. Stillwell from the original scroll received from the Middle East.

1941
'Kia ora' from the No. 3 Section 6th Field Company

This Christmas card, sent from Egypt in 1941, became the impetus for an oral history project that now brings to life the stories of Kiwi engineers during the Second World War.

Among the Kiwi troops training in the shadow of the ancient pyramids at Giza were divisional field engineers or 'sappers', responsible for laying and lifting mines and building and repairing roads and bridges to enable troop movements. At Christmas 1941 this card, drawn by sapper Tom Bell, was produced for the No. 3 Section of the 6th Field Company, showing a pair of soldiers by the pyramid raising a toast to distant New Zealand. The cartoon on the right bears the caption: 'The reason why a camel always has the hump is because it's such a darned long time between drinks.'

The oral history project based around the card was initiated by Lizzie Catherall, the elder daughter of the leader of No. 3 Section, Lieutenant Peter Hamilton, a mining engineer whose father had died in the First World War. Hamilton left New Zealand with the 2nd Echelon of New Zealand troops in early 1940 and didn't return to New Zealand for five years.

Although Catherall's father provided valuable details of his early experiences after joining up in Dunedin in 1939, apart from a few humorous anecdotes he would not talk about his time in North Africa and Italy. Catherall decided to find men who had served with him, to help gain some insight into what he had experienced. Using the names on this Christmas card as a starting point, she gathered 11 oral histories, recording impressions of the life of officers and divisional sappers from the unsuccessful campaigns of Greece and Crete through the action in North Africa and Italy.

In February 2008 Catherall handed over the recordings of the men's stories to the Alexander Turnbull Library's Oral History Section, which contains more than 10,000 items and interviews. The card and other items linked to the participants of the oral history are also to be deposited with the Turnbull.

New Zealand Sapper contribution to WWII oral history project (OHColl-0875) Card courtesy of Lizzie Catherall

To Joan with love
From Peter

*Padre Holland by an improvised altar on the beach at Nofilia, Tripolitania, Libya, during a Christmas Day service for World War 2 New Zealand troops — Photograph taken by CA Churchill 25 Dec 1942
War History Collection
DA-09740*

1942 · CA Churchill
Padre Holland at his altar, Christmas Day, Nofilia, Libya

Christmas 1942 fell in the middle of the pursuit by New Zealand troops of the retreating Germans, following the second battle of El Alamein, in October. The New Zealanders were on the march towards Tripoli in Libya, but a halt was called in order to celebrate Christmas.

Amid the horror and brutality of war, it was the responsibility of the New Zealand army's chaplains to look after the spiritual wellbeing of the troops. A total of 50 chaplains — mostly Church of England, Presbyterian, Roman Catholic and Methodist, plus one each from the Salvation Army, the Baptist Church, the Church of Christ, and the Congregationalists — were assigned to work with troops on active service overseas during the Second World War.

Anglican Padre JT Holland, from Christchurch, was attached to a unit of the New Zealand Army Service Corps, involved in transporting supplies, fuel and ammunition. The army's chaplains had to travel with the soldiers, trying to incorporate ministering to the men around a schedule disrupted by battle and troop movements:

> *Time and again Sundays would be fully occupied in battle or in travelling, and there were few static intervals when religious and recreational activities could be arranged in the evenings . . . In time this travelling life came to have its own clearly marked routine. In the brigade groups the chaplains were able to look after their own units and the other smaller groups that were attached. When Sundays were fully occupied with material affairs it was often possible to hold Church services during the week, and whenever an attack was imminent short pre-battle services would be arranged and Holy Communion administered.*

During Padre Holland's time with the ASC in North Africa he became known for attempting to combat the problem of troops consorting with prostitutes by organising debates on its spiritual and medical dangers. He also served on the hospital ship *Oranje*, carrying wounded and sick soldiers back home to New Zealand.

1943 · George Bull
Maori Battalion Christmas at Maadi Camp, Egypt

A hangi in the desert might be a far cry from a traditional New Zealand Christmas, but to these soldiers at the New Zealand forces' Maadi Camp in Egypt it was a way of making the occasion more reminiscent of home.

New Zealand's Second World War Maori Battalion followed in the footsteps of the Maori Pioneer Battalion that fought in the First World War. Volunteers were called for in October 1939 and the four companies of the Maori (28) Battalion departed for the Middle East in May 1940. In total, 3500 men joined the battalion, of whom 655 died and nearly 2000 were wounded or taken prisoner, in action in North Africa and Italy.

Making a Christmas hangi in the desert became a tradition. This description is of Christmas Day 1942, when the battalion was working to drive the remaining Italian and German troops from North Africa following the battle of El Alamein:

> *Christmas Day was a happy occasion for the Maoris . . . The day opened with a church parade at which Colonel Bennett wished the troops the compliments of the season and mentioned that money had been received from the Maori people which would be distributed equally as soon as it was possible to spend it. 'Hangi' pork and puha gathered from the wadis in the area was the highlight of Christmas dinner and was followed by tinned fruit, cigarettes, a gift parcel from the Patriotic Fund, and letters from home . . .*

The North African variety of puha was not a total success; Captain Pene, who was responsible for its discovery and collection, reminisces:

> *All dixies were commandeered to boil the stuff in (allowing for numerous returns) but, on boiling, the dam stuff smelt like hell — it simply stank. But considering that the only eatables we'd had for weeks resembling 'greens' were dehydrated potatoes and carrot we tucked into the so called puha, smell or no smell.*

The Alexander Turnbull Library holds a collection of wartime images by George Bull, who took these photographs, as well as more than 5500 images taken in New Zealand.

Bull, George Robert, 1910–1966
Uncovering the Christmas hangi at the Maori Training Depot, Maadi Camp, Egypt, 25 Dec 1943
DA-04877-F
Members of the 28th (Maori) Battalion eating hangi-cooked potatoes on Christmas Day, Egypt, 25 Dec 1943
DA-04878-F
Soldier R White with a leg of pork from the hangi at the Maori Training Depot, Maadi, 25 Dec 1943
DA-04879-F
Maori Battalion soldier and dog Paddy the mascot, Christmas Day, Maadi camp, Egypt, 25 Dec 1943
All photographs by George Robert Bull
War History Collection
DA-04880-F

1943
Greetings from NZEF in the Pacific

By Christmas 1943, New Zealand's troops were split between the two ongoing theatres of war: the deserts of North Africa and the jungles of the Pacific.

With the Japanese bombing of Pearl Harbor in December 1941 and the fall of Singapore in February 1942, the war had inched closer and closer to New Zealand. Troops in what would later be the army's Third Division had been sent to Fiji to establish defences in 1940, and coastwatching and radio stations had been established on other islands in 1941. The Japanese continued to advance, however, until the Americans scored vital victories at the battles of Coral Sea and Midway. The Japanese then occupied Guadalcanal in the Solomon Islands, and New Zealand naval, air and army forces became involved, experiencing jungle battle conditions for the first time.

In September 1943, New Zealand ground forces, trained in the bush of the Kaimai Ranges, faced the reality of jungle warfare. Backing up the American forces, they took the island of Vella Lavella, with the loss of 32 men, then Mono and Sterling in the Treasury group, with a further 40 deaths, before capturing the Green Islands group in early 1944.

The National Patriotic Fund Board, for which these cards were produced, was set up in 1939 to raise funds to cover the costs of waging war. Money was to be used to provide recreational facilities and other comforts to soldiers serving overseas and to prisoners of war, administered through organisations such the YMCA, Red Cross and Salvation Army. The board was also given the responsibility of providing for the returning sick and wounded. During the height of the war, from 1942 to 1944, more than £1.8 million was raised.

The artwork on this card is probably by Allan Barclay Barns-Graham.

New Zealand National Patriotic Fund. Greetings from NZEF in the Pacific. Wishing you a happy Christmas and a bright new Year, 1943–1944 / Issued with compliments of National Patriotic Fund Board. 1943.
Colour photolithograph on postcard, 95 x 146 mm
Eph-A-CARDS-Christmas-WWII-1943-02

1943
Dossing Dulcie

Men in drag, a good fairy, elaborate costumes and a grand finale — many of the aspects of a traditional Christmas pantomime can be seen in this photograph. But there's a twist: it was performed by Allied prisoners of war during the Second World War.

First World War veteran Captain Gordon Cowie of Wellington was serving in the 5th Field Regiment of the New Zealand Artillery when he was captured by the Germans in Crete in June 1941 and interned at an officer's camp, or oflag. The prisoners in these camps were not forced to work as regular servicemen were, and were given access to books and encouraged to take part in recreational activities. However, the standard of food and accommodation were often no better than in the work camps.

Around 1700 junior officers were held at Oflag VIIB at Eichstaett, including between 90 and 100 New Zealanders. The camp, set in the Bavarian countryside, was said to have fine grounds, including a sports field and tennis courts for the prisoners' use. As in other camps, a theatre group was set up, with the Germans hiring costumes and props to enable the productions to be staged. Oflag VIIB also had a large library of around 12,000 books. Prisoners were allowed to go on parole walks and were taken to the cinema, and in May 1944 there was a visit to a travelling circus.

Among the plays performed by the camp's theatre group were *Post Mortem* and *The Case of the Frightened Lady* in 1943, and *French Without Tears*, *I Killed the Count* and *Hamlet* in 1944. A musical festival was also held in 1944, with a full choir and orchestra, and in 1945 the New Zealanders dressed as Maori for a revue. As well as its collection of Cowie's photographs of the various plays, many of which were sent home to his wife in Lower Hutt as postcards with no written message, the Alexander Turnbull Library also holds his diary from 1942–45 and a copy of his wartime logbook.

Scene from a play called 'Dossing Dulcie'
1943, photographer unidentified
1 b&w original photographic print(s)
GR Cowie Collection
PAColl-0325-01-1

"Dossing Dulcie" Xmas Panto 1943

Barbed wire Christmas card
1943–1946
From the Ruth Hardcastle Papers
MS-Papers-1441-01

CA 1943
BARBED WIRE HAPPY CHRISTMAS GREETINGS

New Zealanders were sending Christmas cards from the other side of the barbed wire at the Featherston prisoner-of-war camp in the Wairarapa, set up to house around 800 Japanese taken prisoner in the South Pacific.

After several battles in the Pacific and the occupation of Guadalcanal, a POW camp was set up at the request of the American forces on the site of the First World War training camp at Featherston. Some of the prisoners were civilians from work units of the Japanese Imperial Army, while a smaller group were navy, army and air force personnel. Under the terms of the 1929 Geneva Convention the prisoners were required to work during their internment, which at the Featherston camp meant clearing gorse and market gardening.

Fear that the Japanese would invade New Zealand was running high, and racial prejudice boiled over when some of the prisoners went on strike in February 1943. After a confrontation between the 20 or so New Zealand guards and around 240 Japanese, the camp's adjutant fired at the prisoners, who then seemed about to rush the guards. Although no order was issued, the New Zealand guards opened fire. In a burst of fighting that lasted about 30 seconds, 31 Japanese were killed and 91 were wounded, 17 dying later of their injuries. One New Zealander was killed and six injured. The incident was investigated by a military court of enquiry and the New Zealanders exonerated, a decision that was rejected by the Japanese government.

It is not known whether this undated card is from the Christmas before the incident or Christmas 1943, by which time steps had been taken to improve camp morale, including 'a fortnight's holiday from work at Christmas and a supply of ice cream to cheer them at New Year'. Inside the card, signed by Private Ken Death, is a short poem:

A card from 'Little Tokio'
Just to let our friends all know.
We wish them all Good Christmas Cheer
And Happiness and a Bright New Year.

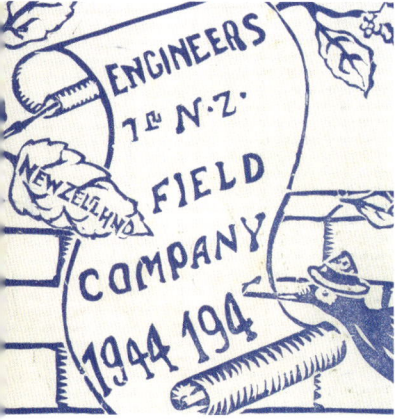

1944
Christmas and New Year greetings from the New Zealand Engineers

By Christmas 1944, the theatre of war for many New Zealand troops had moved from North Africa into Italy. Allied soldiers pushed north to force the Germans to retreat and liberate the Italian people.

The companies of engineers had a vital role to play, disposing of mines and rebuilding roads and bridges so the troops could advance. Much vital infrastructure had been destroyed by shelling from both sides, and army engineers were called in to construct temporary Bailey bridges, clear existing roads and bulldoze new ones, often under enemy fire.

After costly but critical victories in southern Italy, including the Battle of Monte Cassino in April 1944, where at least 350 New Zealand lives were lost, the Allied forces advanced up the Italian peninsula, taking Rome in June. In late 1944 the New Zealand and other Allied troops were attacking German positions along the Gothic Line, north of Florence, capturing Faenza, south of Bologna, on December 14. Having reached the Senio River, the New Zealand troops then hunkered down for a cold, snowy Italian winter — and a proper white Christmas.

The three platoons of the 7th New Zealand Field Company enjoyed a four-course Italian-style Christmas dinner. The menu was printed on the back of this card, with the names of the engineers of the company printed inside. The soup was Taranto Trigno, named after a town and a river in the south of Italy, followed by Morrow cutlets and Gatteo pork and Orsogna lamb, both named after sites of New Zealand engagement. The vegetable options were Rimini Rewi, Fiumecino [sic] cauliflower and Pisciatello peas, followed by Cassino glase (perhaps a glacé) and Empoli Mealia. The wine was Riggiosa, and the meal was followed by nuts and Cappee Rapido coffee, again named after an Italian river.

New Zealand. Army. 2nd NZEF. Engineers. 7th NZ Field Company
Christmas and New Year greetings. 1944-1945.
Relief print, on folded card 220 x 158 mm
Eph-A-CARDS-Christmas-WWII-1944-01

1944 · George Kaye
Soldiers serving Christmas dinner at Faenza, Italy

New Zealand's troops in northern Italy enjoyed a white Christmas in 1944, with the hope that the end of the war was nearly in sight.

The men of the 21st Battalion, stationed near Faenza, south of Bologna, had a quiet Christmas Day, in contrast to the previous weeks of fighting. The official history of the company says snow fell on Christmas Eve, and very few shots were fired on Christmas Day.

> ... the troops in the line had their dinner in peace. It consisted of tinned rations, with each strongpoint providing its own menu, and ran mostly towards soup, oxtail or steak-and-kidney stew, roast pumpkin (scrounged by the troops), plum pudding, oranges, nuts and sweets.

Stephen Llewellyn of the 1st Ammunition Company described Christmas in nearby Forli:

> It was the best Christmas we ever had in the Army. After breakfast — the cooks had been engaged half the night with more important matters and it was a sketchy meal — we paraded outside the officers' mess, with all the bells in Forli ringing their heads off, and marched through the snow to the Esperia Theatre. Here an NZASC carol service was conducted by Padre Holland [see page 146]. The NZASC Band was on the stage and for once in our lives we made no bones about joining in the singing. Before dismissing us the Brigadier congratulated all units on a year's good work and told us to relax and enjoy ourselves ...
>
> Each platoon had made arrangements for a sit-down dinner, and when everything was ready and the great hour arrived how gay and Christmas-like the rooms looked, their walls bright with flags and coloured streamers, their tables with oranges and silver paper and handsome chestnut and amber beer bottles! ...
>
> It is impossible to say what made this particular Natale *so very* buono. Perhaps it was the snow. The quantities of food, of warmth, of wine, of everything. Or perhaps we felt in our hearts that this was the last milestone of its kind in our long journey.

Soldiers of the 21 Battalion serving Christmas dinner, Faenza area, Italy
25 December 1944
Photographer: George Kaye
War History Collection
DA-07996-F

1944 · George Duncan Dunbar Gray
Xmas 1944

Like Gordon Cowie (see page 152), Captain George Duncan Dunbar Gray was destined to spend most of the war in prisoner-of-war camps. He kept an illustrated diary of his internment, from which this cartoon of a prisoners' Christmas comes.

Gray, who was from Wellington, served with the 14th Light Anti-Aircraft Regiment, a division of the 2nd New Zealand Divisional Artillery. He arrived in Egypt in May 1941 but was captured in Libya in November that year, and was held at Modena in Italy and Oflag 79 near Braunschweig (Brunswick) in Germany for the remainder of the war.

Gray's log, held by the Alexander Turnbull Library, tells the story of his internment in cartoonish sketches and brief notes. His sardonic sense of humour is obvious in many of the drawings, including one sketch captioned 'No thanks old man. I gave up eating during the War'. Other entries include a 'joint account list' of rations, notes on rat poison being laid at the camp and a sketch of Judy Garland in *Girl Crazy*, annotated 'Oflag 79 cinema 15/8/44 — first flick since leaving New Zealand 3½ years [ago]'.

From August 1944 until mid-February 1945, as the Allies began to turn the tide on Germany, Gray notes that the prisoners were on half rations, then from February 16 it was 'no parcels, no brews and no fags. German rations reduced 20%. Central heating finished — no fuel. Life bloody.' The prisoners were reduced to a cup of 'ersatz' coffee for breakfast, three small potatoes and hot water for lunch, a cup of mint tea in the afternoon and 'supper: ⅓ bowl watery turnip soup — what a bloody life'.

Oflag 79 was liberated by American troops in April 1945, an occasion sketched by Gray on the last page of his notebook, with the caption 'You bloody beaut'.

The Alexander Turnbull Library collection also includes letters written to Gray by his wife Gay, 'Lady Editor' at Wellington's *Evening Post* newspaper, returned to her stamped 'prisoner of war' and opened by the censor.

Gray, George Duncan Dunbar, b 1906
Xmas 1944.
Coloured pencil drawing on page of notebook, 171 x 122 mm
E-275-061

1945
Greetings from 3 NZ General Hospital

By Christmas 1945 the Second World War was over, and hundreds of New Zealand troops from Europe, the Middle East and the Pacific were being repatriated. These were also the last days of the 3 General Hospital, which was officially disbanded in January 1946.

Medical staff were called up to form the 3 General Hospital in October 1940, and 205 doctors, nurses and auxiliaries left New Zealand for the Middle East with the 4th Reinforcements in February 1941. The hospital was established first in Egypt during the North African campaigns, then moved to near Beirut in Syria and Tripoli in Libya, before moving in September 1943 to Bari, on the Adriatic coast in the south of Italy.

The New Zealanders took over a partially built medical clinic, setting up the surgical division in one of the completed buildings, which they named Tripoli, and finishing off an incomplete block, which they named Beirut, for the medical division. 3 General Hospital became the last link in the chain for evacuating the wounded from Italy, by train or hospital ship.

The hospital was one of the first to experiment with using penicillin to treat wounds. A laboratory was set up and a sample group of soldiers with broken legs, infections, skin grafts and burns were treated. While results were favourable, supplies were short, so the treatment could not be more widely adopted.

This card shows the hospital unit's insignia and motto — a tiki above the words 'Kia kaha', meaning 'Stay strong', in green and red. When the unit left Egypt to move to Syria in 1942, a cast of the emblem was set in the sand beneath the garrison's flagpole as a memento.

3rd New Zealand General Hospital (Bari)
3.N.Z. General Hospital, Kia Kaha.
Greetings 1945–1946.
Relief print on card 120 x 170 mm
Eph-A-CARDS-Christmas-WWII-1945-01

1946–48
JAYFORCE SOLDIERS HOSTING A CHRISTMAS PARTY FOR JAPANESE CHILDREN

Amid the austerity of postwar Japan, occupied by Allied forces, these New Zealand soldiers tried to bring a little Christmas cheer to local children.

The first members of the British Commonwealth Occupation Force arrived in Japan in 1946, drawing on troops from Britain, Australia and India. About 12,000 members of the New Zealand component, called Jayforce, spent up to two and a half years living in Japan following the cessation of hostilities between the Allies and the Japanese in August 1945. The New Zealanders were based at Chofu in the Yamaguchi prefecture, a poor rural area in the southwest of the island of Honshu. Many troops were redeployed from Europe and found conditions in war-ravaged Japan trying, with draughty barracks, poor facilities and food shortages. The occupation was for the most part uneventful, with the only New Zealand casualties arising from illness and accidents.

One of the roles of the BCOF was organising social events for the Japanese people, including Christmas parties like the one pictured here, held by 22 Battalion at Chofu for the children of Japanese workers in the camp. Infantryman SG Breeze wrote home:

> *Last Friday afternoon we put on a party for the Jap children & it turned out quite a success & the children had a great time. They filled themselves until they could not eat any more. All the children were dressed up in the Kimonoes & they looked very pretty . . . Our little company is good with the Japs.*

The last New Zealand members of Jayforce were withdrawn from Japan in September 1948. Servicemen and women who had served solely in Japan were initially denied membership of the Returned Services' Association, as they were not deemed to have been in a war zone. However, this restriction was lifted in 1964.

New Zealand J Force soldiers hosting a Christmas party for Japanese children, Chofu, Japan. Photographer unidentified.
Between 1946–1948
War History Collection
J-0635-F

1950 • *Evening Post*
Sorting the Christmas mail at the General Post Office

December 1950 was a busy season for the mail sorters at Wellington's General Post Office, as captured by an *Evening Post* photographer.

In the 50 years since the Post Office's Christmas card for 1900 (see page 64), the number of items being posted in New Zealand had increased exponentially: from about 53 million items in 1900 to 180 million letters and cards and 386 million total items in 1955. Today, another half-century on and despite the spread of email and the internet, New Zealand Post processes more than a billion items each year, dealing with a stack of mail the equivalent of the height of Mount Cook every day.

The resumption of peace in 1945 had brought new challenges for the postal system. One was a surge in international parcels, as New Zealanders sent much-needed food and other goods to friends and relatives in war-ravaged Britain and Europe. The flood of goods was such that British authorities introduced restrictions: parcels could weigh no more than 11 lb (5 kg), of which only 7 lb (3.2 kg) could be foodstuffs. No one item of food could weigh more than 2 lb (900 g) — unless it was a cake. In the year to March 1948, 12,000,000 lb (5443 tonnes) of parcels were sent to the UK.

The Post and Telegraph Department also had to deal with postwar staff shortages: in 1955 it had 20,000 employees and a whopping 1300 vacancies. While the number of telegrams being sent was declining, the department was also responsible for the burgeoning telephone network. In 1950 more than 50,000 people were added to the network to reach a total of around 257,000 telephone subscribers, with a further 55,000 people on the waiting list. The Post Office of the 1950s also ran a bank, dealt with the registration of births, marriages, deaths and cars, enrolled voters and provided daily weather reports for the Meteorological Office. District postmasters were also legally able to perform marriage ceremonies.

Mail sorters at the General Post Office, Wellington
December 1950
1 b&w original negative(s)
Dry plate glass negative 3.25 x 4.25 inches
Evening Post Collection
114/241/13-G

1950s
CHRISTMAS CARD FROM THE NEW ZEALAND LEGATION, PARIS

This harmless-looking Christmas card featuring the exterior of the New Zealand Legation in Paris is part of one of the most intriguing stories of Cold War espionage. It was sent by New Zealander Paddy Costello and his wife Bil to Doris and Alister McIntosh, while Costello was a diplomat — and possibly a spy — during the 1950s.

Costello was never arrested or openly accused of being a Soviet spy, but rumours about his allegiances abounded both during his life and after his death. Costello was born in Auckland and studied languages at Trinity College, Cambridge, in the 1930s, attending at the same time as infamous British spies-to-be Kim Philby, Guy Burgess, Anthony Blunt and Donald Maclean. After serving in the Second World War, Costello became a diplomat and was stationed at the New Zealand Legation in Moscow for six years before being appointed to the new Paris legation in 1950.

It was while he was working in Paris that the legation issued passports to a Peter Kroger and his wife Helen, allegedly of Gisborne. The pair were later revealed to be Americans Morris and Lona Cohen, high-level KGB agents who had used the New Zealand passports to enter Britain and spy on its nuclear submarine base. The couple had also smuggled plans from the American atomic bomb programme to Moscow. While Costello's connection to the issuing of the passports has never been proven, speculation about his involvement with the Soviets was rife in government and public circles.

Costello left the diplomatic service in 1954 and taught in Manchester until his death in 1964, at the age of 52. James McNeish's book *The Sixth Man*, published in 2007, aimed to shed light on the real story of Costello's life and show that he was not a spy but a victim of the anti-Soviet hysteria of the times.

Cover of Christmas Card illustrated with the New Zealand Legation, Paris
[195-?]
MS-Papers-6759-180-01

1951 • Ian Mackley
Christmas turkeys in Korea

Just a few years after the end of the Second World War, New Zealand troops were once again spending Christmas on the battlefield. This time they were stationed in Korea, where the Cold War had suddenly 'hotted up' with the invasion of South Korea by Communists from the North in June 1950.

The newly formed United Nations called on its members to support South Korea, and within days the New Zealand government had offered naval assistance and, later, ground troops. When volunteers were called for the 1000-strong Kayforce, more than 6000 men came forward within a week.

This picture shows the cooks of 162 Battery and their assistants posing with some of the turkeys for Christmas dinner. In front are Bombardier Rex Gibb from Picton and Gunner Ken Schribber of Taumarunui, and in the back row are Gunners Danny Doyle of Auckland, Les Clark of Belmont, Wellington, and Joe Salt and Alan Kennedy of Christchurch. The photograph was taken by Ian Mackley, a photographer serving with Kayforce who later worked for the *Evening Post* newspaper in Wellington.

Despite the benign weather seen in this image, New Zealand troops found the Korean winter harsh — and a massive contrast to the steamy tropical conditions of summer. The Alexander Turnbull Library holds other images taken on Christmas Day 1951 that show the mess tent of 163 Battery under heavy snow. Wilfrid Poulton, who published his account of his experiences as a serviceman in Korea in 2004, wrote home in early 1953:

> *The temperature was down to -5°[F], i.e. 37° of frost, between Christmas and New Year. George Gillespie's hand stuck to the gun's brake lever and it tore the skin off his palm. I made a note — must use gloves.*

Over three and a half years, around 6000 Kiwis served in Korea, with 43 casualties. An armistice was signed in 1953, but New Zealand troops stayed in Korea as peacekeepers until 1957.

Cooks and assistants of 162 Bty pose with some of the turkeys for the Xmas dinner, 1951. Photographer: Ian Mackley
War History Collection
K-0645-F

1951 • *Evening Post*
Father Christmas goes to the Chatham Islands

Christmas came in force to one of New Zealand's most isolated communities in 1951, with the arrival of a red-suited Santa Claus bearing a sack of gifts.

Duncan Campbell, a reporter with the *Evening Post*, accompanied an unidentified man dressed as Father Christmas on a trip to the Chathams aboard the Solent flying boat *Awatere* in December 1951. The visit was arranged by TEAL, the forerunner of Air New Zealand, to commemorate a year of flights from Wellington to the islands, previously accessible only by boat.

More than 400 people — 80 per cent of the islands' population — turned out at Te Whanga Lagoon to greet Santa as he came ashore by launch, carting a large sack of toys. Gifts were handed out from beneath two large Christmas trees and from 'lucky dip'-style bran tubs set up on the beach. The *Evening Post* recorded:

> *In the three and a quarter hours he distributed good cheer, the islanders — all in paper hats provided by TEAL — consumed several bottles of whisky and soft drinks, numerous cartons of strawberries, 48 dozen chocolate ice creams, 60 dozen ice cream blocks, and 10 gallons of ice cream, estimated to produce 450 ices. The ice cream was donated by a Christchurch firm and carried free by TEAL.*

The collection of photographs of the trip held by the Alexander Turnbull Library includes several taken on board the flying boat of a sheepdog that broke out of its crate during the flight, 'to investigate his surroundings in a passenger compartment which had been converted for the carriage of innumerable crates of bananas, sausages and other goods'. Among the other passengers on the flying boat were 'the well-known footballer, Russell Hohaia, of Taranaki, and Myra Tuuta, of Big Bush, who were going to the Chathams to be married from Myra's home'.

Father Christmas goes to the Chatham Islands, Dec 1951
Evening Post *Collection*
(left to right) 114/408/56-F, 114/408/43-F, 114/408/38-F, 114/408/48-F

1953 • *Photo News*
Scene at Tangiwai after the railway disaster

Christmas 1953 was memorable in New Zealand for two major events: the visit of the newly crowned Queen Elizabeth II (see page 176) and the horrific railway accident at Tangiwai on the Central Plateau.

At 3 pm on Christmas Eve, 1953, the daily express from Wellington to Auckland headed off from the capital, laden with 285 passengers setting out on their annual holidays. Little did they or the train's driver know that at 10.21 pm it would plummet into the flooded Whangaehu River at Tangiwai, after a bridge weakened by the passing of a volcanic lahar collapsed beneath the train's weight.

The lahar, a mass of water, ice and mud from the crater lake of Mount Ruapehu, had flowed down the path of the river about half an hour before the train arrived. The wave of water, estimated to be around 6 m high, took out the large concrete piers and steel girders of the Tangiwai bridge, leaving only the railway tracks remaining in place. When the engine, pulling nine passenger cars and two vans, reached the river, the rails simply buckled.

The engine plunged into the river at such a speed it nearly reached the opposite bank, 35 m away. Six carriages followed, their passengers either crushed by the impact or swept away down the swollen river. Many bodies could not be identified or were carried down the river and out to sea. Miraculously, the last three carriages stayed on the tracks on the southern bank.

In total, 151 people were killed in the accident — at the time New Zealand's fourth-worst disaster (after the wreck of the *Orpheus* in 1863, the 1931 Hawke's Bay earthquake and the Tarawera eruption of 1866) and the eighth-largest railway disaster in world history. A mass funeral service for unidentified victims was held in Wellington on New Year's Eve, attended by the Duke of Edinburgh.

Scene at Tangiwai after railway disaster
Dec 1953
Gelatin silver print 15.3 x 20.9 cm
Photograph by Photo News Ltd
PAColl-2388-06

1953
THE QUEEN'S CHRISTMAS AT GOVERNMENT HOUSE

The tragedy at Tangiwai (see page 174) threatened to overshadow the visit of the young Queen Elizabeth II to New Zealand, the first ever by a ruling monarch to this country.

The Queen and the Duke of Edinburgh spent Christmas 1953 at the then Government House (now the Staff Common Room at the University of Auckland). The royal couple had arrived in New Zealand by sea two days earlier, and were preparing to tour the country. Their visit was met with almost hysterical adulation, with massive crowds turning out to see the new monarch, crowned just six months earlier. It was estimated that two out of every three New Zealanders (out of a population of around two million) saw the queen during her five-week nationwide tour.

The monarch's Christmas Day began with Holy Communion at the private chapel of the Bishop of Auckland, before a return to Government House where she and the Duke were serenaded with carols by the Friendly Road children's choir. Then Santa arrived, his sleigh drawn by a team of Shetland ponies, with gifts for the royal couple and their children: Prince Charles, then aged five, and Princess Anne, three, who had been left behind in England during the southern hemisphere tour. There was a train set for Prince Charles and a doll's wardrobe for Princess Anne. The Queen was presented with a diamond-studded fern-leaf brooch by Lady Allum, 'on behalf of the women of Auckland', and the Duke of Edinburgh received a gold pen and pencil set.

The royal couple then attended another service, at the Cathedral of St Mary in Parnell, before a traditional lunch at Government House and a sightseeing drive around Auckland's suburbs. In the evening, the Queen made her first annual Christmas broadcast from Government House — the only time she has given the broadcast from outside the United Kingdom — departing from her original script at the end to make reference to the Tangiwai disaster and express her condolences.

Their Royal Highnesses Queen Elizabeth II, and the Duke of Edinburgh, during Christmas, Government House, Auckland Dec 1953. Photographer unidentified. 1/2-035247-F

1955
JAMES SMITH'S CHRISTMAS CORNER

A generation of Wellington children have fond memories of the annual Christmas windows at the James Smith department store. The unveiling of each year's windows and their nightly showing was a highlight throughout the 1950s.

James Smith Ltd
Albums showing shop window displays
1951–1965
Photograph by KE Niven Ltd
PA1-o-791-43

The first Christmas window display was installed in 1951, telling the tale of 'Janet and John in the Land of Christmas Dreams', using dolls, mannequins, elaborate backdrops and props to tell a story through a sequence of seven large display windows. The windows were put together entirely by James Smith staff, who even wrote the stories, often in rhyming verse. Advertising for the windows noted that they were 'a purely entertainment display with no merchandise included'.

The windows, and their grand unveiling, quickly became a Christmas institution. In 1952 the theme was The Teddy-Bears' Picnic, with an 'Under the Sea' theme in 1954 and a more traditional nativity series in 1955, telling 'The Christmas Story' complete with plastic-doll angels and lots of tinsel.

A working model train was installed for the 'Puffin' Billy Christmas Express' windows in 1956 and the displays became futuristic in 1957, with the unusual combination of 'Noddy in Space'. A newspaper story of the time noted that:

Noddy's clothes were also patterned on the premises, but, as they were assembled by mere males, they lack the proper finishing touch — the seams are glued instead of sewn!

The windows fronted onto the intersection of Cuba and Manners streets. The building's art deco facade and the name James Smith's Corner remain Wellington landmarks, but the department store itself closed in 1993.

The Alexander Turnbull Library holds two albums of photographs and newspaper clippings relating to the Christmas windows, annotated by a staff member involved in creating the displays, as well as albums of photographs of the company's popular Christmas parades from the 1960s to the 1990s.

Out Side Display 1955...

☆ "Your Christmas Shopping Corner"... ☆ "Your Christmas Shopping Corner"...
..James Smith's Corner..

87

1956–57 • AVIS ACRES
HUTU AND KAWA

The iconic red flowers of the New Zealand Christmas tree, pohutukawa, were brought to life in a series of children's books written and illustrated in the 1950s by Avis Acres.

Acres, born Thyra Avis Mary McNeill in Wellington in 1910, began her career as an artist when her family moved to Auckland. Forced to leave school after the collapse of a business venture of her father's, she did some commercial drawing work and studied sketching at night school.

Acres and her husband Bob moved to Taupo in 1950 and it was there that she invented the flower fairies Hutu and Kawa, inspired by Australian artist May Gibbs's 'gumnut babies', Snugglepot and Cuddlepie. Acres produced a comic strip featuring Hutu and Kawa, and their bush friends such as Willy Weka, as well as other more European-style pixies and elves, for *The New Zealand Herald*'s children's page for a decade. She also wrote three books about their adventures: *Hutu and Kawa Find an Island* (from which this illustration comes), *The Adventures of Hutu and Kawa* (in which they ride a kiwi) and *Hutu and Kawa Meet Tuatara*, in which they help a tuatara find a new home.

Acres also published a book about Opo, the dolphin at Opononi, in 1956. Although she wrote no more books, she continued to paint and write about nature for the rest of her life.

Acres was a conservationist and a keen observer of nature. The illustrations in the Hutu and Kawa books feature much ecological detail and the text often carries conservation messages; in *Hutu and Kawa Find an Island*, for example, the fairies meet their cousin Rata and the story highlights the impact of possums on native vegetation.

The Alexander Turnbull Library holds the original watercolours for many of the Hutu and Kawa illustrations, as well as paintings for her bird books.

Acres, Avis 1910–1995
"We must be cousins!" said Hutu.
[1956–57].
Watercolour, 380 x 286 mm
B-087-021
© Avis Acres Estate

1957 • E Mervyn Taylor
Tui or parson bird

Although best known for his illustrative work, especially in the *School Journal*, artist E Mervyn Taylor also turned his hand to more commercial work, including this tui Christmas card for Mr and Mrs T Wallace Dick of Wellington in 1957.

Taylor was born in Auckland in 1906. He trained as a jewellery engraver then worked in advertising before setting up as a freelance artist in 1939. After serving in the Second World War he got a job with the School Publications Branch of the Department of Education and began producing wood engravings to illustrate the *School Journal*.

This then became his predominant artistic style, and before his death in 1964 he created more than 200 woodblocks, as well as working in watercolour and sculpture. His highly recognisable woodcuts of native flora and fauna, Maori life and legends, and historical scenes have become classics of their time. In addition to his illustrative work, which was exhibited internationally, he was also commissioned to create a number of murals.

This card was produced by the Mermaid Press, set up by Taylor and friends, including the poet and printer Denis Glover, in Wellington in 1953. The company published a book of Taylor's work in 1957, as well as his linocuts of animals for children and ranges of Christmas cards.

On the back of this card is a description of the tui, 'about the size of an English blackbird but . . . not jet black because its feathers reflect metallic colours . . . It is a great mimic, a famous songster and a skilful acrobat in the air.'

Taylor, Ernest Mervyn 1906–1964
Tui or parson bird. Wellington, Mermaid Press [1950s?]
Photolithograph of wood engraving 110 x 75 mm
E-279-q-005
© Terence Taylor

Tui or Parson Bird   E. Mervyn Taylor

CA 1957 • EILEEN MAYO
WITH GOOD WISHES TO YOU FOR CHRISTMAS AND THE NEW YEAR

This print by British-born artist Eileen Mayo uses areas colour and its absence to illustrate the contrasts between the northern hemisphere Christmas of her early life and the summer festival of her life Down Under.

Mayo was born in Norwich in England, and studied wood engraving and theatrical design at the Slade School of Art at the University of London, and sculpture with Henry Moore at Chelsea Polytechnic. She also studied in France, and had a wide range of artistic interests, from printmaking to tapestry.

She emigrated to Australia in 1952 and taught at the National Art School in Sydney, while exhibiting widely. She created several murals, wrote for the *Sydney Morning Herald* and designed posters, stamps and coins. This Christmas card was made during her time in Australia, when she was living in Neutral Bay, Sydney.

In 1962, after the break-up of her marriage, she moved to New Zealand to join her mother and sister who had lived in New Zealand since the 1920s. She continued printmaking and stamp design, including designs for the 1970 standard denominations issue, featuring moths and fish, the 1971 UNICEF and Antarctic Treaty commemorative stamps, and a 1972 issue on alpine flowers, all featuring her distinctive printmaking style and bright colours.

At the time, Mayo described stamp designing as 'very satisfying', adding, 'Stamps last. If you paint a picture only a few people see it, but stamps circulate.' In 1966 she was invited to submit coin designs for the issue of decimal currency. Mayo also taught at the University of Canterbury School of Fine Arts, and was made a Dame Commander of the British Empire shortly before her death in 1994.

Mayo, Eileen Rosemary (Dame), 1906–1994
With good wishes to you for Christmas and the New Year. [Between 1953 and 1962. Christmas card with two hands]
Woodcut on folded card, 131 x 108 mm
B-131-06-010

1959 · George Poppleton rumming the Christmas pudding, Campbell Island

*Bob Lamb and Bob Rae rumming the Christmas pudding, Campbell Island 1959. Photography by PG Poppleton
PG Poppleton Collection
PA12-1424-030*

Deep in the subantarctic, the men stationed at the meteorological station on Campbell Island at Christmas 1959 had to make their own fun, as well as their own pudding.

George Poppleton first went to Campbell Island, 700 km southeast of the South Island, in 1955 as the leader of a team of men stationed there to take meteorological observations for the Civil Aviation Administration. The team spent a year maintaining Tucker Camp, inland from Perseverance Harbour in the centre of the island, and preparing a site for a new camp to be built in preparation for increased scientific activity during the International Geophysical Year 1957–58. They also had to make scientific observations of weather conditions and the ionosphere, and observe the aurora australis, or southern lights, when visible.

Poppleton returned to the island as team leader for a further two years from the summer of 1958. During this time he took a large number of photographs, most of which were developed on the island, including this photograph of cook Bob Rae (right) and meteorological observer Bob Lamb adding a little something extra to the pudding.

In 2000 Poppleton published a book based on his diaries from his time on Campbell Island, including a description of Christmas on the island in 1959. Meteorological observer Henry Cousins made a souvenir menu for the nine men, decorated with a pen-and-wash drawing of a Campbell Island flowering plant. Cousins also translated the menu into French, 'but don't ask me what we ate that day, as my knowledge of the French language is still adrift', Poppleton wrote.

Despite the isolated nature of the celebration, Poppleton's description of Christmas Day had a universal theme:

> *Bob Rae surpassed himself with the spread he put on. It would have been as good a meal as anyone, anywhere sat down to that day . . . We ate too much and sat or lay around for the rest of the afternoon.*

1963
CHRISTMAS MENU, THE HERMITAGE

This Christmas celebration was one of the first at the Tourist Hotel Corporation's 'new' Hermitage Hotel at Mount Cook, where guests were encouraged to enjoy the festivities 'thousands of feet above worry level', according to its slogan at the time.

The slogan was somewhat ironic, as the THC had recently had more than its share of serious worries. The previous Hermitage building had been destroyed by fire just after renovations were completed in 1957, and in the same year storms and torrential rain had seriously disrupted the South Island tourist season. Just three years earlier the THC's Franz Josef hotel had also burnt down.

The first Hermitage, built in 1884, was just a cob hut at the end of a two-day coach journey from the railway terminus at Fairlie in the Mackenzie Basin. After being destroyed by floods it was replaced by a grander building in 1914, and the Hermitage became a popular destination. Because of its key position as one of the jewels in the crown of the burgeoning tourist industry, after the Hermitage's destruction in 1957 a new hotel was hastily constructed, with builders working 12-hour days in bad weather to enable the hotel to reopen in May 1958. Designed in the modernist style, it was described by British architectural expert Nikolaus Pevsner as one of the finest buildings in New Zealand.

In 1963 Christmas guests could enjoy a comprehensive menu of seasonal delights, including traditional dishes such as turkey with cranberry sauce and chipolatas, Canterbury lamb with wild mint jelly, roast suckling pig with cider apple conserve, and poached chicken with Albufera sauce. There were also the cold buffet options of Melton Mowbray pork pie, baked ham, Timaru crayfish in the shell and pressed ox tongue in aspic, as well as the favourite Kiwi salads of asparagus spears, marinated beetroot, sliced tomato and onion rings, and lettuce and egg with oil mayonnaise. Guests could enjoy Veuve Clicquot Ponsardin champagne and Châteauneuf-du-Pape, or McWilliams New Zealand Bakano, one of the first red wines to be produced commercially in the Hawke's Bay.

Tourist Hotel Corporation
Gala. Christmas dinner, The Hermitage, Mount Cook . . . Wednesday, 25th December, 1963. [Menu cover].
Photolithograph, coloured, 273 x 178 mm
Eph-B-HOTEL-Mt-Cook-1963-01
© Hermitage Hotels

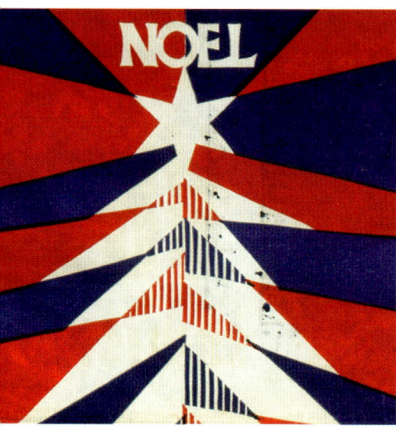

1963 • DON RAMAGE
A CHRISTMAS SEASON OF *CASSE-NOISETTE*

The ballet known in English as *The Nutcracker* is a perennial Christmas favourite, but December 1963 was the first time local audiences had seen it performed by the New Zealand Ballet. This season at the Grand Opera House in Wellington also featured the world premiere of *The Winter-Garden*, written and choreographed by New Zealanders.

The New Zealand Ballet was founded in 1953 by Danish immigrant Poul Gnatt, who had arrived in New Zealand in 1952 and set about establishing a professional company. Gnatt not only directed the ballet but also designed and made costumes for the fledgling troupe, while the dancers themselves set up the stage and lighting, packed and unpacked props and scenery, and drove themselves around the country to perform.

In 1962 Russell Kerr, a New Zealand dancer and choreographer who had spent several years performing in Europe in the 1950s, was appointed artistic director of the company. In 1963 he choreographed productions of *Concerto* and *Balesque* before this production of *Casse-Noisette*, which became one of the company's most popular touring shows in the coming years.

The ballet, first performed in St Petersburg in 1892 with music by Tchaikovsky, tells the story of Clara Stahlbaum, who is given a beautiful painted nutcracker at her family's grand Christmas party. She and her brother fight over the nutcracker and it gets broken. Later that night Clara sneaks out of bed to sleep beneath the Christmas tree, where the nutcracker comes to life and takes her on a series of adventures.

Playing the Nutcracker Prince in this production, sharing the role with Terence James, was a young Jon Trimmer, now Sir Jon and one of New Zealand's best-known dancers. To celebrate his 50 years with the company in 2008, he performed the title role in a touring season of *Don Quixote*.

The stylised Christmas tree on the cover of the programme and other publicity was designed by Don Ramage, a modernist graphic designer, artist and printmaker.

Ramage, Donald, 1923–
New Zealand Ballet. Noel. Casse Noisette.
Christmas season. Opera House December 2nd to 7th [1963].
Screen print on poster 758 x 253 mm
Eph-D-CABOT-Dance-1963-01
© Don Ramage

1964 · Russell Clark
'Behold I bring you good tidings of great joy'

December 1964 marked the 150th anniversary of the first official Christmas in New Zealand: the delivery of a service by the Reverend Samuel Marsden at Rangihoua in the Bay of Islands (see page 122).

This image shows Marsden giving his famous sermon from a makeshift pulpit, starting with Psalm 100 and followed by a passage from the Bible, Luke 2:10: 'Behold I bring you good tidings of great joy'. Pictured at Marsden's right is the Ngapuhi chief Ruatara, who acted as interpreter for the first Christmas service, and the two Maori in regimental uniform in the centre of the painting are Korokoro and Hongi Hika, under whose protection the mission at the Bay of Islands would fall after Ruatara's death just a few months later. At the front of the crowd are a small group of missionaries: Thomas Kendall, John King and William Hall, and their families.

This painting by Russell Clark was originally reproduced in the 1948 edition of *Holly Leaves*, the Christmas annual of the *Illustrated Sporting and Dramatic Review*, a weekly tabloid published in London, as part of a special supplement focusing on historical events. This version was reprinted in 1964 by the New Zealand Church Missionary Society to commemorate the 150th anniversary of the first New Zealand Christmas. According to the artist, the original watercolour had been destroyed.

Clark was an artist, painter and sculptor perhaps best known for his illustrations in the *School Journal* and *New Zealand Listener* during the 1940s and 50s. He served as a war artist in the Pacific during the Second World War as well as teaching at the Canterbury University School of Art and creating several large public murals and sculptures. He had a distinctive, robust style and is well known for his depictions of Maori people, inspired by several visits to the Urewera in the 1950s.

Clark, Russell Stuart 1905–1966
Samuel Marsden's first service in New Zealand. The Gospel of Jesus Christ first proclaimed on these shores by the Rev. Samuel Marsden at Oihi, Bay of Islands, Christmas Day, 1814 [Christchurch] N.Z. Church Missionary Society [1964]
Photolithograph 304 x 279 mm
B-077-006

(By courtesy of the artist, Russell Clark.)

"BEHOLD I BRING YOU GOOD TIDINGS OF GREAT JOY"

Thus was the Gospel of Jesus Christ First Proclaimed on these Shores by the Rev. Samuel Marsden at Oihi, Bay of Islands, Christmas Day, 1814

N.Z. CHURCH MISSIONARY SOCIETY

1968 • Willow Macky
Pohutukawa Carol

With lyrics written by a homesick chaplain in the North African desert and a tune by one of New Zealand's most prolific folk song writers, the *Pohutukawa Carol* deserves to be a New Zealand classic.

The words to the carol were written by Father Ted Forsman, a Catholic priest and Second World War army chaplain, while on active service in the Libyan desert in late 1941 (see page 146). During the fighting between British and Allied troops and the German Afrika Korps, led by General Erwin Rommel, Forsman was taken captive with the medical unit to which he was attached. With little food and water, and in the middle of a desert battle, Forsman and the six other chaplains worked hard to minister to the wounded until the camp was freed a week later.

Despite the extreme conditions, Forsman was moved to write poems about his experiences in battle, and what became the *Pohutukawa Carol* was one of them. Forsman drew on his memories of the large pohutukawa trees on his family's land at Pakuranga, Auckland, at what was then called Barn Beach, now Half Moon Bay.

The poem was set to music in 1968 by Willow Macky, a prolific songwriter who is perhaps best known for her carol *Te Harinui*. Macky, who died in 2006, specialised in writing folk songs about New Zealand history, people and events, including Maori legends. She chose to write about New Zealand topics after finding a lack of folksongs about her own country, and produced more than 113 songs, 92 lyrics and a folk opera called *The Maori Flute*, as well as more than 300 poems.

This version of the *Pohutukawa Carol* was first performed at the King's School carol service, held at St Matthew-in-the-City, Auckland, on December 8, 1968. A note with the handwritten score says it was performed by boys with guitar accompaniment, and that it may be sung in two-part harmony or raised half a tone if wished.

Macky, Willow, Music scores, J– P
1957–1986
96-331-9/10
© Willow Macky Estate

POHUTUKAWA CAROL.

Words by Fr. Forsman
Music by Willow Macky

1. Now crimson, crimson Christmas trees, Pohutukawas rim our seas, And flowering, flame on every shore, For joy of Him whom Mary bore. Babe so poor and small, Jesus, God of all, O with us a-bide, This ho-ly Christmas-tide.

CAROL A POHUTUKAWA CAROL
(Words by Father Forsman, Music by Willow Macky, 1968)

Now crimson crimson Christmas Trees,
   Pohutukawas rim our seas,
And flowering, flame on every shore,
   For joy of Him whom Mary bore.

Babe so poor and small
Jesus God of all
O with us abide
This holy Christmas-tide.

Such trees gave wood to make his cot,
   And all his toys from wood he got,
And when he came to ply a trade,
   He shaped from trees the things he made.

Because a tree had brought us doom,
   Was Jesus born of Mary's womb,
To blossom high on Calvary's tree,
   The crimson bloom that makes us free.

Long raise, O trees, about our land,
   Your crimson sign on every hand,
That we may tell each Christmas morn,
   Why Jesus was of Mary born.

From: King's School Carol Service, 1968.

1968 · *Evening Post*
Audience in the Majestic Theatre, Wellington

The Christmas treat for many young Wellingtonians and their parents in 1968 was a trip to see *Finian's Rainbow*, the last film musical to star Fred Astaire.

This audience, photographed at the Majestic Theatre, was comprised of the winners of an *Evening Post* competition offering tickets to a special preview of the movie, the Majestic's special Christmas attraction. The caption described the crowd of 1000 as 'a sight not seen in a Wellington picture theatre since the days of the Hopalong Cassidy and Sitting Bull epics'.

Finian's Rainbow, starring Astaire, Petula Clark and Tommy Steele, was a film adaptation directed by a young Francis Ford Coppola of a 1947 musical. It told the story of Irishman Finian McLonergan (Astaire) and his daughter Sharon (Clark), who emigrate to the United States with a magical pot of gold, which Finian plans to bury in the ground so it will grow. However, he is pursued by a leprechaun (Steele) and also gets into trouble with a bigoted local senator. It was 69-year-old Astaire's first musical for 11 years, and its mixture of fantasy and social satire received mixed reviews.

The Majestic, in Willis St, was one of the largest cinemas in Wellington, seating more than 2000 people. According to cinema historian Wayne Brittenden, when it opened in 1925 it was considered 'the last word in grandeur' with its floodlit exterior, huge lobby, Doric columns and giant dome over the auditorium. Its heyday continued into the 1940s, under the ownership of Kerridge Theatres, and its cabaret lounge was popular during the Second World War. Brittenden notes, however, that 'after the advent of television its size became untenable, as audiences declined markedly. In its later years it sometimes endured the indignity of double features'. The theatre closed in 1984 and was demolished in the pre-crash building boom of 1987 to make way for the new Majestic Centre.

Audience in the Majestic Theatre, Wellington
7 December 1968
Cellulose triacetate negative, 35 mm
Dominion Post *Collection*
EP/1968/5341/1F

1970 · CHARLES FLEMING
SAVE MANAPOURI

As well as sending good wishes for the festive season, Christmas cards can also be used to convey a wider message, as in this card from scientist and conservationist Sir Charles Fleming and his wife Peg.

The Manapouri power scheme in Fiordland became a hot political topic in 1969, and was one of the first major environmental causes in this country. The government proposed to raise the level of the lake by up to 30 m to create greater pressure to drive the underground power station between the lake and Doubtful Sound. The plan initially encountered opposition only from locals, but it became a matter of national concern; in 1970 more than quarter of a million New Zealanders — almost 10 per cent of the population — signed a petition against the project. The development became a key election issue in 1972, and the new Labour prime minister Norman Kirk delivered on his promise to save the lake.

It was natural that the Flemings would be outspoken against the raising of Manapouri. One of New Zealand's leading twentieth-century scientists, Sir Charles Fleming was a geologist and ornithologist who specialised in biogeography: the study of the sequence of settlement of plants and animals, and the development of our native flora and fauna. He formed the Ornithological Society of New Zealand and was twice president of the Royal Society of New Zealand. He was active in a number of conservation campaigns and organisations, including Save Manapouri, the Native Forests Action Council and the Royal Forest and Bird Protection Society.

The Flemings issued a hand-made Christmas card each year, usually featuring a montage of images and notes about family activities. The Alexander Turnbull Library holds a collection of these dating from the 1950s to the 1980s, including this card showing an Australasian crested grebe or kamana swimming on Lake Manapouri.

Fleming, Charles Alexander (Sir), 1916–1987
Once to every man and nation comes the moment to decide . . . Save Manapouri. Christmas and New Year greetings from Peg and Charles Fleming, and Jean.
December 1970
Photolithograph, black and white,
124 x 156 mm (folded)
A-304-006
© Mary McEwen

1974 • Beverley Shore Bennett
Epiphany window design, Holy Trinity, Devonport

This stained-glass window design for a historic Auckland church depicts one of the most familiar aspects of the Christmas story — the visit of the three wise men from the East to the baby Jesus.

The window was installed in Holy Trinity, Devonport, on Auckland's North Shore, in 1976 and was dedicated at the farewell service for outgoing vicar the Reverend Lin Dawson. Installed in the south transept of the historic timber Gothic church, it has four panels and depicts the Virgin Mary with the infant Christ on her knee, with Joseph on the right and the Magi at the left. At the top are angels, a crown of thorns, a chalice, a chi-rho symbol and a crown.

The window was fabricated by Miller Studios in Dunedin, which at the time specialised in stained-glass work. The Epiphany window is notable because its detail is fully painted, the most expensive technique for creating stained glass.

The first church on the Holy Trinity site, near the Devonport waterfront, was a combined chapel and school built with the help of the British Navy in 1856, when the tiny settlement was known as Flagstaff. A new church was built in 1865, then the current kauri Holy Trinity church, designed by architect Edward Bartley, was built in two stages in the 1880s. The church also has two other windows designed by Shore Bennett: the West Window, installed in 1987 for the church's centenary and showing Christ in glory, and the north-transept Resurrection Window, installed in 1997.

Shore Bennett trained as a portrait painter in Wellington and at the Byam Shaw School of Art in London, in the 1950s. In the 1960s she turned to stained-glass work and church embroidery, and was made the first lay canon of Wellington Cathedral in recognition of her ecclesiastical art and design work. The Alexander Turnbull Library holds a large collection of Shore Bennett's stained-glass designs, including windows for the Anglican cathedrals in Wellington and Napier.

Shore-Bennett, Beverley, ca 1930–
'Epiphany'; proposed design for Holy Trinity Devonport. South transept. 1974.
Watercolour, arch-shaped,
on sheet 386 x 279 mm
A-325-026
© Beverley Shore Bennett

"Epiphany"
Proposed design for
Holy Trinity
Devonport.
South Transept.

Beverley Shove Bennett
A.M.G.P.
Miller Studios Ltd. 1974.

1975 • SID SCALES
SEASON OF PEACE AND GOODWILL

This satirical Christmas card from 1975 shows the unmistakable face of prime minister Robert Muldoon and Federation of Labour president Tom Skinner alternating as the lion and the lamb.

The caricatures were drawn by Sid Scales, who was cartoonist for the *Otago Daily Times* for 30 years from 1951. Scales started his career in newspapers as a cadet journalist on the *Timaru Herald* at the age of 17. He moved to Christchurch with the aim of becoming a commercial artist four years later, but joined the air force at the outbreak of the Second World War. He spent some time as a prisoner of war in Java, and on his return to New Zealand he used rehabilitation bursaries granted to returned servicemen to study at the Canterbury School of Art and the Central School of Art in London. Scales then set up a commercial art business in Christchurch, but was wooed to the *Otago Daily Times* and remained there for the rest of his working life, producing around 6000 cartoons.

During the 1970s Muldoon was one of Scales's favourite subjects and this cartoon was published just a week after Muldoon's first National government was sworn in. Muldoon was an outspoken, irascible politician who came to power in a period of economic turmoil and set about trying to fix it by somewhat extreme means, including imposing wage and price freezes to try to halt inflation. Arguing the toss was the Federation of Labour, representing the highly unionised workforce. In January 1976, the government ordered a 3.2 per cent general wage increase, despite an 8.1 per cent rise in the cost of living. Muldoon notes dryly in his autobiography:

> *We had had straight-from-the-shoulder talks with the Federation of Labour, the Combined States Services Organisation and the employers prior to the Christmas break, and the wage order was accepted without too much complaint — somewhat, I must admit, to my surprise.*

This card was one of a collection of cartoons belonging to Muldoon himself, donated to the Alexander Turnbull Library by his widow, Dame Thea, in 1993.

Scales, Sidney Ernest 1916–2003
Wage order postponed till late in January . . .
19 December 1975
Ink and crayon on card, 262 x 348 mm
A-291-034
© Ngaire Scales

1977 • *Evening Post*
Start of the school holidays

No matter how much a child likes going to school, the start of the Christmas holidays is always an occasion for celebration.

These children running out the school gate with blatant disregard for road safety were pupils at Karori Normal School in Wellington. They had probably also been chanting the refrain, popular with schoolchildren for many years:

No more homework
No more books
No more teachers' dirty looks!

Unlike their counterparts in the northern hemisphere, New Zealand school pupils have always had the advantage of Christmas celebrations and the long summer holiday falling at the same time. By the 1970s the six weeks of Christmas school holidays usually started in mid-December, with a return to classes in late January — just when the weather was coming right.

These kids may also have been rushing home to catch the 1977 *Nice One* Christmas special on TV, featuring host Stu Dennison — widely known for his thumbs-up pose, Chopper bicycle and catchphrase 'Nice one' — and a well-coiffed Roger Gascoigne. The comedy and musical variety show included guest appearances from TV personalities Selwyn Toogood, Bob Parker and Brian Edwards.

Karori Normal School is one of Wellington's oldest schools. It was established as Karori Village School in 1857 and moved to its current site in Donald St in 1875. Kathleen Beauchamp, who grew up to be well-known short-story writer Katherine Mansfield, attended the school from 1895–98, and the school's grounds feature a birdbath as a memorial to her.

Karori Normal School children taking off
for the holidays
15 December 1977
1 b&w original negative(s) Single image on
35 mm negative strip
The *Dominion Post* Collection
EP/1977/5055/8-F

1992 • CHRIS SLANE
CHRISTMAS DAY IN AUCKLAND

By the end of the twentieth century, the traditional Christmas dinner had often been set aside in favour of a more summery repast: a barbecue. But if you live in Auckland, chances are that at least at some stage during the day, it's going to rain.

As this book shows, there has been a diversity of experiences of Christmas in the two centuries since Europeans first settled here. Approaching the second decade of the twenty-first century, New Zealand's increasing ethnic diversity and secular way of life ensures that, as in the past, there is no one 'New Zealand Christmas' but a range of ways to celebrate and commemorate the day with family and friends — even if it is just a day's respite from the Christmas rush before the Boxing Day sales.

I chose this image to end the book for two reasons: firstly, because it seemed to me to encapsulate the current classic Kiwi Christmas. I also chose it because, growing up, the Christmas holidays for me meant going to our bach at Scandretts Bay on the Mahurangi Peninsula, north of Auckland.

Chris Slane's parents and mine were friends, and they had a bach in the next bay over. Chris, some years older than my sister and me, was a somewhat mysterious young man who sometimes deigned to speak to us. Including his cartoon here is a nod in the direction of our shared experiences of Christmas holidays in the north in the 1970s.

Slane is now a well-known freelance cartoonist and illustrator, a regular contributor to the *New Zealand Listener*, *Metro* and *The Shed* magazines. This cartoon was drawn for the Auckland law firm Cairns Slane, where Chris's father Bruce was a partner until his appointment as Privacy Commissioner in 1992. As commissioner, he continued to issue cards drawn by his son until his retirement from that office in 2003.

Slane, Chris. Christmas cartoons, ca 1992
A-296-004/006
© Chris Slane

References

Books

Clarke, Alison, *Holiday Seasons: Christmas, New Year and Easter in nineteenth-century New Zealand,* Auckland University Press, Auckland, 2007.

Downes, Peter, *Shadows on the Stage: theatre in New Zealand — the first 70 years,* John McIndoe, Dunedin, 1975.

Griffith, Penny, Ross Harvey and Keith Maslen (eds), *Book & Print in New Zealand: a guide to print culture in Aotearoa,* Victoria University Press, Wellington, 1997 (also online at *www.nzetc.org/tm/scholarly/name-121550.html*).

Keith, Hamish, *The Big Picture: a history of New Zealand Art from 1642,* Random House New Zealand, Auckland, 2007.

King, Michael, *New Zealanders at War,* Heinemann, Auckland, 1991.

Maddock, Shirley and Michael Easther, *A Christmas Garland,* William Collins Publishers, Auckland, 1980.

McClure, Margaret, *The Wonder Country: making New Zealand tourism,* Auckland University Press, Auckland, 2004.

McCormick, EH, *Portrait of Frances Hodgkins,* Auckland University Press, Auckland, 1981.

Olssen, Erik and Marcia Stenson, *A Century of Change: New Zealand 1800–1900,* Longman Paul, Auckland, 1989.

Platts, Una, *Nineteenth Century New Zealand Artists: a guide & handbook,* Avon Fine Print, Christchurch, 1980. (also online at *www.nzetc.org/tm/scholarly/tei-PlaNine.html*)

Pope, Diana and Jeremy, *Mobil New Zealand Travel Guide: North Island,* 7th edition (revised), Reed, Auckland, 1991.

Priestley, Rebecca and Veronica Meduna, *Atoms, Dinosaurs and DNA: 68 great New Zealand scientists,* Random House New Zealand, Auckland, 2008.

Rogers, Anna and Max Rogers, *Turning the Pages: the story of bookselling in New Zealand,* Reed, Auckland, 1993.

Smith, Paul, *New Zealand at War: World War II, the New Zealand Perspective,* Hodder Moa Beckett, Auckland, 1995.

Stenson, Marcia, *Illustrated History of New Zealanders at War,* Random House New Zealand, Auckland, 2008.

Wolfe, Richard, *Battlers, Bluffers and Bully-Boys: how New Zealand's Prime Ministers have shaped our nation,* Random House New Zealand, Auckland, 2005.

Websites

Auckland Art Gallery, *www.aucklandartgallery.org.nz*
Dictionary of New Zealand Biography, *www.dnzb.govt.nz*
New Zealand History Online (Ministry of Culture and Heritage), *www.nzhistory.net.nz*
NZ Post stamp information, *http://stamps.nzpost.co.nz*
Papers Past (National Library), *http://paperspast.natlib.govt.nz*
Tapuhi (National Library), *http://tapuhi.natlib.govt.nz*
Te Ara, the Encyclopedia of New Zealand, *www.teara.govt.nz*
The Endeavour Journal of Joseph Banks online, *http://southseas.nla.gov.au/journals/banks/contents.html*
Timeframes (National Library), *http://timeframes.natlib.govt.nz*

Specific entries

2 [Chevalier]. Day, Melvin N, *Nicholas Chevalier, Artist: His life and work,* Millwood Press, Wellington, 1981; **5** [Ladye Birds]. *http://homepages.ihug.co.nz/~melbear/century2.htm*; **6** [Thomas E Price]. *www.wairarapamaori.com*; Bagnall, AG, *Wairarapa: A Historical Excursion,* Hedley's Bookshop, Masterton, 1976; **7** [Backhouse]. Norton, Maurice, *Soldier, Settler, Artist: JP Backhouse* (self-published booklet); **9** [Bullock Webster]. Bullock-Webster, Harold, *From the Hudson's Bay Company to New Zealand,* Whitcombe and Tombs, Auckland, 1938; **12** [Tarawera eruption] Conly, Geoff, *Tarawera: the destruction of the Pink and White Terraces,* Grantham House, Wellington, 1985; Ell, Gordon, *Volcanoes and Thermal Wonders,* The Bush Press of New Zealand, Auckland, 2004; **14** [Emily Harris]. Dawson, Bee, *Lady Painters: the flower painters of early New Zealand,* Viking, Auckland, 1999; **21** [Lands and Survey] *http://www.surveyors.org.nz/Documents/PART%20IV%20THE%20PIONEER%20LAND%20SURVEYORS%20OF%20NEW%20ZEALAND.pdf*; **22** [Boer War]. Crawford, John with Eileen Ellis, *To Fight for the Empire: an illustrated history of New Zealand and the South African war, 1899–1902,* Reed, Auckland, 1999; **23** [HG Robley]. Bellamy, Allan, ed., *Horatio Gordon Robley: soldier artist in the Bay of Plenty, 1864–1866,* Tauranga Historical Society, Tauranga, 1990; **24** [Remembrance flashed . . .]. Wilson, AC, *Wire and Wireless: a history of telecommunications in New Zealand, 1890–1987,* The Dunmore Press, Palmerston North, 1994; **26** [Fern card]. *www.archives.govt.nz/exhibitions/currentexhibitions/makingourmark/index.php?page=unofficiallynz*; **28** [DIC]. Laurenson, Helen B, *Going Up, Going Down: the rise and fall of the department store,* Auckland University Press, Auckland, 2005.; **29** [GPO]. *www.jeffpylenz.com/Jeffs-blog/WEB/Benoni%20White%20postcards.htm*; **30** [Auckland Weekly News]. Scholefield, GH, *Newspapers in New Zealand,* AH & AW Reed, Wellington, 1958; **31** [Winkelmann]. Edwards, Vivien, *Winkelmann: images of early New Zealand,* Benton Ross, Auckland, 1987; **33** [Campbell & Ehrenfried]. McLauchlan, Gordon, *The Story of Beer: beer and brewing — a New Zealand history,* Penguin Books, Auckland, 1994; **34** [Seddon]. Boon, Kevin, *The Liberals,* Waiatarua Publishing, Auckland, 2005; *http://library.christchurch.org.nz/Heritage/Exhibitions/1906/Introduction/*; **35** [Godber]. *www.rimutaka-incline-railway.org.nz/*; Cameron, Norman, *Rimutaka Railway,* New Zealand Railway and Locomotive Society Inc, Wellington, 1992; **38** [Christmas cheques]. *www.mch.govt.nz/coat-of-arms.htm#history*; **39** [TSS *Ulimaroa*]. *http://mns.ewebs.com/index.php?id=13,0,0,1,0,0*; Plowman, Peter, *Ferry to Tasmania: a short history,* Rosenberg Publishing, New South Wales, 2004; **41** [Letter to Santa]. 'Dear Santa', *Contact,* December 21, 1999; **42** [Maymorn]. Lawson, Will, *Historic Trentham, 1914–1917: the story of a New Zealand military training camp, and some account of the daily round of the troops within its bounds,* Wellington Publishing Co, Wellington, 1918; McGibbon, Ian, ed., *The Oxford Companion to New Zealand Military History,* Oxford University Press, Melbourne, 2000; **45** [Sling Camp]. Gallahar, Laeonie, *The Chalk Kiwi*, *www.armymuseum.co.nz/museum-news/acquisitions.html*; Jim Fuller, *http://archiver.rootsweb.ancestry.com/th/read/SUSSEX-PLUS/2001-01/0979080862*; **46** [A right loyal greeting]. Sinclair, Keith, *A Destiny Apart: New Zealand's search for national identity,* Allen & Unwin, Wellington, 1986; **52** [Diggers]. *www.army.mil.nz/our-army/structure/uniforms/ceremonial-service-dress.htm*; *www.diggerhistory.info/pages-uniforms/nz-slouch.htm*; **53** [Quick March]. *www.rsa.org.nz/remem/rsa_hist_90years.html*; **54** [Christmas fairy]. *http://www.daao.org.au/main/read/2804*; **55** [Sleeping Beauty]. Harding, Bruce, 'Ngaio Marsh, 1895–1982', in *Kōtare 2007,* Special Issue — Essays in New Zealand Literary Biography — Series One: 'Women Prose Writers to World War I', Victoria University of Wellington, Wellington, 2007 (online at *www.nzetc.org/tm/scholarly/tei-Whi071Kota-t1-g1-t10.html*); Harcourt, Peter, *A Dramatic Appearance: New Zealand Theatre 1920–1970,* Methuen Publications, Wellington, 1978; **56** [Robert Field]. Fraser, Ross, 'Robert Nettleton Field', *Art New Zealand,* No. 19, Autumn 1981; Dunn, Michael, *New Zealand Painting: a concise history,* Auckland University Press, Auckland, 2003; **57** [Health stamps]. Tennant, Margaret, *Children's Health, the Nation's Wealth: a history of children's health camps,* Bridget Williams Books, Wellington, 1994; **58** [Reed]. McLean, Gavin, *Whare Raupo: the Reed Books story,* Reed, Auckland, 2007; **61** [Rail timetable]. *www.nzmaritime.co.nz/earnslaw.htm*; Churchman, Geoffrey B and Tony Hurst, *South Island Main Trunk,* IPL Books, Wellington, 1992; **63** [David Low]. Seymour-Ure, Colin and Jim Schoff, *David Low,* Secker and Warburg, London, 1985; **66** [Evans Bay Carnival]. *www.adb.online.anu.edu.au/biogs/A140367b.htm*; **67** [Toy hospital]. King, Michael, *The Penguin History of New Zealand,* Penguin Books, Auckland, 2003; Sinclair, Keith, *A History of New Zealand* (revised edition), Penguin Books, Auckland, 1988; **70** [Padre Holland]. Underhill, Rev. ML, Squadron Leader JMS Ross, Sydney D Waters and Rev. NE Winhall, *Chaplains,* Historical Publications Branch, Wellington, 1950 (online at *www.nzetc.org/tm/scholarly/tei-WH2Chap.html*); **71** [Maori Battallion]. Cody, Joseph F, *28 Maori Battalion,* Historical Publications Branch, Wellington, 1956 (online at *www.nzetc.org/tm/scholarly/tei-WH2Maor.html*); **72** [NZEF in the Pacific]. Taylor, Nancy M, *The Home Front,* Volume I, Historical Publications Branch, Wellington, 1986 (online at *www.nzetc.org/tm/scholarly/tei-WH2-1Hom.html*); **73** [Dossing Dulcie]. Hall, DOW, 'Prisoners of Germany', in *Episodes & Studies,* Volume 1, Historical Publications Branch, Wellington, 1948 (online at *www.nzetc.org/tm/scholarly/tei-WH2-1Epi-_N95731.html*); Mason, W Wynne, *Prisoners of War,* Historical Publications Branch, Wellington, 1954 (online at *www.nzetc.org/tm/scholarly/tei-WH2Pris.html*); **74** [Featherston]. Mason, W Wynne, *Prisoners of War* [see 72]; **76** [Faenza]. Cody, Joseph F, *21 Battalion,* Historical Publications Branch, Wellington, 1953 (online at *www.nzetc.org/tm/scholarly/tei-WH2-21Ba.html*); Llewellyn, SP, *Journey Towards Christmas: Official History of the 1st Ammunition Company, Second New Zealand Expeditionary Force, 1939–45,* Historical Publications Branch, Wellington, 1949 (online at *www.nzetc.org/tm/scholarly/tei-WH2Chri.html*); **77** [Gray]. *http://riv.co.nz/rnza/units/14laa/thornton.htm*; Murphy, WE, *2nd New Zealand Divisional Artillery,* Historical Publications Branch, Wellington, 1966 (online at *www.nzetc.org/tm/scholarly/tei-WH2Arti.html*); Mason, W Wynne, *Prisoners of War* [see 72]; **78** [3 General Hospital]. McKinney, JB, *Medical Units of 2 NZEF in Middle East and Italy,* Historical Publications Branch, Wellington, 1952 (online at *www.nzetc.org/tm/scholarly/tei-WH2MMed.html*); **79** [Jayforce]. Brocklebank, Laurie, *Jayforce: New Zealand and the military occupation of Japan 1945–48,* Oxford University Press, Auckland, 1997; Gillespie, Oliver A, *The Pacific,* Historical Publications Branch, Wellington, 1952 (online at *www.nzetc.org/tm/scholarly/tei-WH2Paci.html*); **80** [Christmas mail]. Robinson, *A History of the Post Office in New Zealand,* Government Printer, Wellington, 1964; *www.nzpost.co.nz*; **81** [Costello]. McNeish, James, *The Sixth Man: the extraordinary life of Paddy Costello,* Random House New Zealand, Auckland, 2007; **82** [Kayforce]. Boag, Stuart (ed.), *Ice and Fire: New Zealand and the Korean War, 1950–1953,* Agenda, Wellington, 2000; Poulton, Wilfred, *K Force in Korea: a soldier's life in the 16th New Zealand Field Regiment,* Wilfred Poulton, Palmerston North, 2004; **84** [Tangiwai]. Conly, Geoff and Graham Stewart, *Tragedy on the Track: Tangiwai and other New Zealand Railway Accidents,* Grantham House, Wellington, 1986; Hardingham, John, *The Queen in New Zealand* [see 85]; **85** [Queen]. Davies, Valerie, *Royal Tours: 100 years of royal visits to New Zealand,* Random House New Zealand, Auckland, 1989; Hardingham, John, *The Queen in New Zealand,* AH and AW Reed, Auckland, 1954; **86** [James Smith]. *www.wellington.govt.nz/services/heritage/pdfs/artdeco.pdf*; **87** [Hutu and Kawa]. *www.reed.co.nz/profiled.cfm?viewauthor=1*; **88** [E Mervyn Taylor]. James, Bryan, *E Mervyn Taylor, Artist: Craftsman,* Steele Roberts, Wellington, 2006; **89** [Mayo]. McGahey, Kate, *The concise dictionary of New Zealand artists: painters, printmakers, sculptors,* Gilt Edge, Wellington, 2000; **90** [Campbell Island]. Poppleton, George, *Campbell Island 1955–1956, 1958–60,* Jenn Falconer, Wellington, 2001; **92** [Royal New Zealand Ballet]. *www.nzballet.org.nz*, *www.nutcrackerballet.net*, Ashton, Beatrice, *The New Zealand Ballet: the first twenty-five years,* Association of Ballet and Opera Trust Boards, 1978; **93** [Russell Clark]. Dunn, Michael, *The Drawings of Russell Clark, New Zealand Artist and Illustrator,* William Collins, Auckland, 1976; **94** [Pohutukawa Carol]. Underhill, Rev. ML, Squadron Leader JMS Ross, Sydney D Waters and Rev. NE Winhall, *Chaplains* [see 70]; *http://sounz.org.nz/contributor/composer/1173*; *www.catholicremuera.org.nz/theme/Revelations%20november%202007.pdf*; **95** [Majestic Theatre]. *www.imdb.com*; Brittenden, Wayne, *The Celluloid Circus: The Heyday of the New Zealand Picture Theatre 1925–1970,* Random House New Zealand, Auckland, 2008; **96** [Save Manapouri]. *www.meridianenergy.co.nz/AboutUs/PowerStations/Manapouri*; **97** [Beverley Shore Bennett]. Shore Bennett, Beverley, *A Key to Embroidery,* Black Robin, Wellington, 1986; Spackman, Murray (ed.), *Parish of the Holy Trinity, Devonport, New Zealand: centenary, 1856–1956,* Holy Trinity Anglican Church, Devonport, 1990; *www.millerstudios.co.nz/services.asp*; *www.holytrinity.gen.nz/Pages/StainedGlass.htm*; **98** [Sid Scales] *www.library.otago.ac.nz/hocken/exhibitions/scales.html*; Reid, John and Mark Winter, *Laughing Lines: 12 New Zealand contemporary cartoonists,* Pilgrims South Press, Dunedin, 1981; Muldoon, RD, *Muldoon,* AH & AW Reed, Wellington, 1977; **99** [Karori school]. *www.kns.school.nz*; *tvnzondemand.co.nz*